USDA

United States
Department of
Agriculture

Forest Service

Pacific Northwest
Research Station

General Technical
Report
PNW-GTR-864

October 2012

Natural and Cultural History of Beargrass (*Xerophyllum tenax*)

Susan Hummel, Sarah Foltz-Jordan, and Sophia Polasky

Authors

Susan Hummel is a research forester, U.S. Department of Agriculture, Forest Service, Pacific Northwest Research Station Forestry Sciences Laboratory, 620 SW Main Street, Suite 400 Portland, OR 97205; **Sarah Foltz-Jordan** is a conservation associate, Xerces Society for Invertebrate Conservation, 628 NE Broadway, Suite 200, Portland, OR 97232; and **Sophia Polasky** is a forestry technician, U.S. Department of Agriculture, Forest Service, Pacific Northwest Research Station, Forestry Sciences Laboratory, 3200 SW Jefferson Way, Corvallis, OR 97331.

Cover photograph by Frank Lake.

Natural and Cultural History of Beargrass (*Xerophyllum tenax*)

Susan Hummel, Sarah Foltz-Jordan, and Sophia Polasky

U.S. Department of Agriculture
Forest Service
Pacific Northwest Research Station
Portland, Oregon
General Technical Report PNW-GTR-864
October 2012

Published in cooperation with:
The Xerces Society for Invertebrate Conservation
Portland, Oregon

Abstract

Hummel, Susan; Foltz-Jordan, Sarah; Polasky, Sophia. 2012. Natural and
cultural history of beargrass (*Xerophyllum tenax*). Gen. Tech. Rep. PNW-
GTR-864. Portland, OR: U.S Department of Agriculture, Forest Service,
Pacific Northwest Research Station. 80 p.

Beargrass (*Xerophyllum tenax* (Pursh) Nutt.) is a source of food, habitat, and raw
material for animals, pollinating insects, and people across its range in the Western
United States. The plant has long been used by Native Americans, who harvest
the leaves for basketry and other crafts. More recently, beargrass has become
an important component of international trade for the commercial floral greens
industry. Changes in natural and anthropogenic disturbances are occurring within
the range of beargrass, including fire frequency and severity, plant harvest intensity,
and land use. This report documents how changes in disturbance patterns might
affect beargrass and its associated ecosystem diversity, identifies gaps in knowledge
or potential conflicts in human use, and records quantitative and qualitative information on the natural and cultural history of beargrass. We list and discuss some
key sociocultural, environmental, and economic issues that relate to managing
beargrass and the forested ecosystems in which it grows. These include a lack of
information on the main factors affecting beargrass reproduction and persistence,
including the importance of pollinators and light environment on plant fitness;
differences in desired leaf properties sought by traditional and commercial harvesters; and inconsistent documentation on the volume and properties of harvested
beargrass in total and by harvester group. Future research needs include advanc-
ing knowledge of the effects of human and natural disturbances on the plant and
its habitat, including silvicultural practices, leaf harvest practices, and fire (both
prescribed and wild).

Keywords: Beargrass, *Xerophyllum tenax*, community diversity, forest management, floral greens, basketry, fire pollination ecology, reproductive strategies.

Contents

Introduction

Beargrass (*Xerophyllum tenax* (Pursh) Nutt.) is a source of food, habitat, and raw material for animals, pollinating insects, and people across its range in the Western United States (fig. 1). Some of its colloquial names hint at its many virtues: bear lily, deer grass, elk grass, pine-lily, soap grass, Indian basket grass, American grass, and western turkeybeard. Beargrass is a herbaceous, perennial monocot with long, fibrous, evergreen leaves and a succulent rhizome. The flowers are displayed on a distinctively tall stalk (fig. 2). The plant has long been used by Native Americans, who harvest the leaves for basketry and other crafts. More recently, beargrass has become an important component of international trade for the commercial floral greens industry.

Changes in natural and anthropogenic disturbances are occurring within the range of beargrass, including fire frequency and severity, plant harvest intensity, and land use. This report will document how changes in disturbance patterns might affect beargrass and its associated ecosystem diversity, identify gaps in knowledge or potential conflicts in human use, and record quantitative and qualitative information on the natural and cultural history of beargrass. Such information is prerequisite to informed research and management of the ecosystems in which beargrass grows.

Beargrass Characteristics

Taxonomy and Nomenclature

Beargrass is not a true grass but is classified as a lily (order Liliales). It is in the Melanthiaceae family, together with the genera *Trillium* and *Paris*, which differ morphologically from beargrass (Rudall et al. 2000). Only two members of the *Xerophyllum* genus exist. The congeneric *Xerophyllum asphodeloides* (L.) Nutt.— or eastern turkeybeard—is restricted to the Southeastern United States. Eastern turkeybeard is similar to beargrass in form, but is smaller than beargrass in both basal area and size of flower, or inflorescence (Rentz 2003). Beargrass is not listed as a threatened plant (Higgins et al. 2004, Maule 1959, Rentz 2003, USDA FS 2011), whereas eastern turkeybeard is classified as threatened in Tennessee and rare in Georgia (USDA FS 2011).

The scientific name of beargrass is derived from Greek: *xeros* (dry), *phyllon* (leaf); and Latin: *tenax* (grasping, tenacious) (Hitchcock and Cronquist 1973). Its prevaling common name is derived from being a food source for bears (Crane 1990).

1

Figure 1—Map of beargrass global range, showing two disjunct distributions.

Figure 2—Beargrass (*Xerophyllum tenax*) in flower.

Morphology and Reproduction

Beargrass is a herbaceous, rhizomatous plant with a perennial mass of narrow, long, basally clustered leaves (Hitchcock and Cronquist 1973). The plant can reproduce both vegetatively (by sprouting from the rhizome) and sexually (by flowering).

The rhizome is a tuberous, semiwoody rootstock, 1 to 2 cm thick with cord-like roots (Hitchcock and Cronquist 1973, Maule 1959). Each vegetative shoot arises from the upper surface of the rhizome at the leaf base (Crane 1990). The basal leaves are tough, fibrous and wiry and occur in large clumps (Hitchcock and Cronquist 1973, Pojar and MacKinnon 1994). Beargrass leaves can be 15 to 100 cm long and 2 to 10 mm wide at their base, decreasing in width to a thin, stiff, wiry tip (Maule 1959, Rentz 2003, Vance et al. 2001). Leaves typically have one series of unbranched parallel veins, with a keeled rib-line and edges that are rough and finely toothed (Rentz 2003). The stem leaves are much shorter than the basal leaves (Pojar and MacKinnon 1994). The leaves of beargrass are typical of xerophytic plants in that they have a thickened cuticle and restriction of stomata to the lower leaf surface. Such adaptations minimize water loss during periods of drought (Rentz 2003). In addition, a thick-walled epidermis provides beargrass with insulation and contributes to its frost tolerance (Rentz 2003).

When flowering, beargrass produces a single, erect, unbranched flowering stalk that bears a dense, terminal inflorescence of 50 to 400 flowers (Munger 2003, Vance et al. 2001) (fig. 2). The flowers mature successively from the bottom to the top, so that midway through the flowering season (approximately May–August), the raceme appears as a conical or cylindrical cluster of opened flowers topped by unopened floral buds (Maule 1959, Vance et al. 2004). The lily-like flowers are approximately 1.3 cm across, white to cream colored, with six distinct tepals (Munger 2003). The ovaries are three-celled (Hitchcock and Cronquist 1973). Each flower has six stamens with long violet filaments and yellowish pollen released on the anthers (Hitchcock and Cronquist 1973, Vance et al. 2001). There is no conspicuous difference in pollen morphology between beargrass and eastern turkeybeard (Takahashi and Kawano 1989). Pollen size is reported as 22.6 by 29.0 μm in the major axis of the ellipse and 14.9 by 19.9 μm in the polar axis (Takahashi and Kawano 1989). Floral nectar is not present at any stage in the floral lifespan of beargrass (Vance et al. 2004), and floral scent is variable. For example, Vance et al. (2004) reported that one-fifth of the beargrass flowers in their sample had a sweet smell like cultivated lilacs (*Syringa*), while the remaining four-fifths smelled musty-acrid.

Beargrass fruits are three-lobed, ovoid, acute, dry capsules, generally about 5 to 7 mm in length (Hitchcock and Cronquist 1973, Pojar and MacKinnon 1994). Vance et al. (2004) found that the fruits contained an average of seven seeds. Crane (1990) reported that beargrass seeds are approximately 4 mm long and average about 830,000 per pound (about 1,830,000 per kilogram). Mature seeds are light tan in color (Wick et al. 2008).

Plant Growth and Development

Plants (and individual leaves) may live for several years, producing vegetative growth and offshoots (Rentz 2003, Vance et al. 2004). Death of a plant is reported to occur upon flowering (Hitchcock and Cronquist 1973), but because vegetative reproduction (offshoot production from the rhizome) occurs before flowering, the plants are persistent and long lived (Crane 1990, Laursen 1984). The phenology of this plant (growth, development, and response to changing climate) is not well studied. Empirical evidence is lacking if leaving tillers during leaf harvest prevents subsequent flowering of the plant.

Vegetative reproduction generally takes place between spring and summer (Peter and Shebitz 1996) and may occur throughout an individual's lifespan (Crane 1990). Field observations suggest that sprouting of the rhizome may be increased by habitat disturbance, including fire and timber harvest (Crane 1990, Shebitz et al. 2009, Thomas and Schumann 1993). Rhizomes are capable of sprouting following severe disturbance and can be relocated by high-elevation mudflows and debris slides (Adams et al. 1987).

The onset and length of flowering in beargrass appears to differ with differences in soil temperature, aspect, canopy cover, and elevation. Flowering has been reported as early as April (Vance et al. 2004), and as late as September (Maule 1959). Anthesis (the period of time during which the flower is fully expanded so pollination can occur) is successive along the peduncle. It begins with the most basal flowers in the raceme and progresses upward; the same inflorescence may have receptive flowers for up to 2 weeks, while each individual flower is receptive for only a few days (Vance et al. 2004). Fruit set begins in mid-summer (July), and mature seeds dehisce in late summer (Crane 1990, Vance et al. 2004).

In some beargrass populations, flowering occurs in cycles (5- to 7-year) and can be synchronous throughout the population, while at other sites, flowering is sporadic (Crane 1990, Rentz 2003). At experimental sites in Mount Rainier National Park, Washington, profuse blooming was reported to occur almost every year, and low flower abundance was the exception rather than the norm (Maule 1959). The observed variability in flowering patterns is not well understood, but may be related to site-specific environmental conditions (Crane 1990).

The relative importance of vegetative vs. sexual reproduction varies with habitat characteristics. Flowering in beargrass has been reported to be most prevalent in plants growing in the open, or in forest gaps, and is less frequent as the forest canopy recloses (Crane 1990, Maule 1959, Vance et al. 2004). In a study in Mount Rainier National Park, Maule (1959) speculated that the amount of light reaching the plant was "the most obviously important [factor] in bringing about flowering." In her study, no beargrass plants were observed blooming in deep shade (although old flowering stalks were present), and all flowering plants were confined to open meadows, forests with filtered light, and shrub-covered areas. Similarly, experimental manipulations of beargrass habitat by Shebitz et al. (2009a) found that both flowering and vegetative reproduction (shoot production) increased in areas where vegetation and coarse woody debris were manually cleared. Low temperatures, particularly soil temperatures, also may inhibit flowering, even independent of light environment. Maule (1959) examined soil temperatures of flowering and nonflowering plants at 34 stations in Mount Rainier National Park and found that soil temperatures around the roots of flowering plants (at a depth of 7.6 cm) were between 0.5 to 2.5 °C higher than those beneath nonflowering plants in the same vicinity with approximately the same amount of moisture and sunlight. At only two of the stations were the root temperatures of flowering and nonflowering plants the same, and in no case was root temperature of a nonflowering plant found to be higher than a flowering one. Competition for water or nutrients may also be a factor.

Topography, humus content of the soil, and ground cover characteristics may also influence soil temperature and affect flowering patterns. As with many plants, beargrass flowering tendencies may be influenced by the length and warmth of the growing season of the previous year when the flower buds were formed (Maule 1959). Overall, vegetative reproduction is reported to occur more frequently than flowering (Vance et al. 2001).

Cultivation

Beargrass is considered difficult, but possible, to cultivate (Vance et al. 2001). Wild-collected seeds may be sown either in greenhouses or in the wild; both wild-harvested and greenhouse-grown seedlings can be transplanted (Vance et al. 2001, Wick et al. 2008). In contrast, offshoots and mature plants collected from the wild can fail to establish in containers or be successfully transplanted (Vance et al. 2001, Wick et al. 2008). Wild seeds are generally collected in late August and early September when capsules turn tan and open (Wick et al. 2008). Both wild-collected seeds and greenhouse-grown plants are commercially available.

Beargrass seed requires cold stratification for germination (Crane 1990), and a 14-week cold stratification period has been successfully used (Shebitz et al. 2009b). Based on a greenhouse study of seed germination, the same study recommended soaking beargrass seeds for 24 hours in smoke-infused water prior to sowing (Shebitz et al. 2009b). Because beargrass is mycorrhizal, it may require soil with appropriate fungi for growth (Vance et al. 2001), and a significant increase has been observed in first-year seedlings that were given a mycorrhizal inoculant (Wick et al. 2008). A detailed propagation protocol is provided by Wick et al. (2008).

Range

Beargrass is restricted to western North America and has two disjunct distributions: one maritime extends north from west-central California through Oregon to the Olympic Peninsula and Cascade Mountains in northwestern Washington; the other extends north from Wyoming to Canada along the Rocky Mountains (Crane 1990, Maule 1959, Vance et al. 2001) (fig. 3). In the maritime distribution, beargass occurs sparingly near sea level in the coastal region, from Monterey County in west-central California to northwestern Washington, and again just below the summits of the Coast Range mountains over almost the same latitudinal range. In the Sierra Nevada and Cascade Range, it is found from Placer County, California, northward about 700 miles to Stampede Pass, Washington, and ranges in elevation from approximately 610 to 2134 m (2,000 to 7,000 ft) (Higgins et al. 2004, Maule 1959). In the continental distribution, beargrass it grows at elevations between 610 to 2134 m (Maule 1959).

Habitat

Beargrass is an early to late-successional pioneer species that inhabits a wide variety of habitat types, including woodlands, clearings, meadows, bogs, slopes, ridges, coniferous forests, and nonforested, steep talus slopes (Vance et al. 2001). It can be a significant component of subalpine meadows (Shebitz et al. 2008), and also can dominate the understory of dry, mixed-coniferous forest types (Higgins et al. 2004). It is found at highest density under canopy openings in various forest types. Lists of plants associated with beargrass are provided in tables 1 and 2 (Crane 1990). Beargrass is adapted to harsh environmental conditions, such as low nutrient levels, low moisture levels, and cold weather conditions (Rentz 2003). Crane (1990) described beargrass communities and site characteristics, in the two distributions, as follows:

Figure 3—Documented beargrass locations (Maule 1959).

Table 1—Tree, shrub, and herbaceous plant species reported to grow in association with *Xerophyllum tenax* (note: list is not exhaustive)

Species	Common name	Reference
Trees:		
Abies amabilis	Pacific silver fir	Crane 1990
Abies grandis	Grand fir	Crane 1990
Abies lasiocarpa	Subalpine fir	Crane 1990
Abies shastensis	Shasta red fir	Crane 1990
Arbutus menziesii	Pacific madrone	Peter and Shebitz 2006
Pinus contorta	Lodgepole pine	Peter and Shebitz 2006
Pinus monticola	Western white pine	Crane 1990
Pseudotsuga menziesii	Douglas-fir	Peter and Shebitz 2006
Salix scouleriana	Scoulers willow	Peter and Shebitz 2006
Thuja plicata	Western redcedar	Schlosser and Blatner 1997
Tsuga heterophylla	Mountain hemlock	Vance et al. 2001
Tsuga mertensiana	Western hemlock	Schlosser and Blatner 1997
Abies lasiocarpa	Subalpine fir	Vance et al. 2001
Abies procera	Noble fir	Vance et al. 2001
Shrubs:		
Arctostaphylos uva-ursi	Kinnikinnick	Peter and Shebitz 2006
Arctostaphylos x media	Manzanita	Peter and Shebitz 2006
Mahonia aquifolium	Hollyleaved barberry	Peter and Shebitz 2006
Eriophyllum lanatum var. *lanatum*	Wooly sunflower	Peter and Shebitz 2006
Gaultheria shallon	Salal	Peter and Shebitz 2006
Goodyera oblongifolia	Western rattlesnake plantain	Peter and Shebitz 2006
Holodiscus discolor	Oceanspray	Peter and Shebitz 2006
Kalmia microphylla	Western swamp laurel	Shebitz 2005
Ledum groenlandicum oeder	Labrador tea	Shebitz 2005
Lonicera ciliosa	Orange honeysuckle	Peter and Shebitz 2006
Menziesia ferruginea	Fool's huckleberry	Schlosser and Blatner 1997
Paxistima myrsinites	Oregon boxleaf	Peter and Shebitz 2006
Rhododendron macrophyllum	Pacific rhododendron	Peter and Shebitz 2006
Rosa gymnocarpa	Dwarf rose	Peter and Shebitz 2006
Symphoricarpos hesperius	Trailing snowberry	Peter and Shebitz 2006
Vaccinium caespitosum	Dwarf bilberry	Peter and Shebitz 2006
Vaccinium ovatum	California huckleberry	Peter and Shebitz 2006
Vaccinum sp.	Whortleberry	Vance et al. 2001
Herbs:		
Achillea millefolium var. *occidentalis*	Western yarrow	Peter and Shebitz 2006
Agrostis pallens	Seashore bentgrass	Peter and Shebitz 2006
Allotropa virgata	Sugarstick	Peter and Shebitz 2006
Anemone lyallii	Little mountain thimbleweed	Peter and Shebitz 2006
Antennaria howellii spp. *neodioica*	Howell's pussytoes	Peter and Shebitz 2006
Apocynum androsaemifolium	Spreading dogbane	Peter and Shebitz 2006

Table 1—Tree, shrub, and herbaceous plant species reported to grow in association with
***Xerophyllum tenax* (note: list is not exhaustive) (continued)**

Species	Common name	Reference
Boschniakia hookeri	Vancouver ground cone	Peter and Shebitz 2006
Cyperaceae family	Sedges	Vance et al. 2001
Camassia quamash var. *azurea*	Prairie camas; blue camas	Shebitz 2005
Campanula scouleri	Pale bellflower	Peter and Shebitz 2006
Castilleja hispida	Harsh Indian paintbrush	Peter and Shebitz 2006
Danthonia spicata var. *pinetorum*	Poverty oatgrass	Peter and Shebitz 2006
Erythronium oregonum	Giant white fawnlily	Peter and Shebitz 2006
Festuca roemeri	Roemer's fescue	Peter and Shebitz 2006
Fragaria virginiana ssp.	Virginia strawberry	Peter and Shebitz 2006
Fritillaria affinis	Checker lily	Peter and Shebitz 2006
Iris tenax	Toughleaf iris	Peter and Shebitz 2006
Lilium columbianum	Columbian lily	Peter and Shebitz 2006
Linnaea borealis	Twinflower	Schlosser and Blatner 1997
Lupinus albicaulis	Sicklekeel lupine	Peter and Shebitz 2006
Lupinus latifolius	Broadleaf lupine	Peter and Shebitz 2006
Luzula multiflora	Common woodrush	Peter and Shebitz 2006
Packera macounii	Siskiyou mountain ragwort	Peter and Shebitz 2006
Polystichum munitum	Western swordfern	Peter and Shebitz 2006
Pteridium aquilinum	Western brackenfern	Peter and Shebitz 2006
Ruppertia physodes	Forest scurfpea	Peter and Shebitz 2006
Ranunculus occidentalis var. *occidentalis*	Western buttercup	Peter and Shebitz 2006
Rubus ursinus	California blackberry	Peter and Shebitz 2006
Solidago simplex ssp. *simplex* var. *simplex*	Mount Albert goldenrod	Peter and Shebitz 2006
Trillium ovatum	Pacific trillium	Peter and Shebitz 2006
Viola adunca var. *adunca*	Hookedspur violet	Peter and Shebitz 2006

Table 2—Plants associated with beargrass (Kuchler classification)

Plant association	Kuchler classification
California mixed-evergreen forest	K029
Cedar-hemlock-pine forest	K013
Douglas-fir forest	K012
Fir-hemlock forest	K004
Grand fir–Douglas-fir forest	K014
Lodgepole pine–subalpine fir forest	K008
Mixed-conifer forest	K005
Silver fir–Douglas-fir forest	K003
Western spruce–fir forest	K015

Source: Crane 1990.

West Coast sites—

In the Coast Range of Oregon, beargrass is found on steep sites on well-drained, frequently shallow soils on rugged, rocky topography near ridgetops. In the Cascade Range, it may be dominant on cold dry ridges and mountain tops ranging in elevation from 1433 to 1768 m (4,700 to 5,800 ft) with soils that are poorly drained in spring and excessively well drained in summer. In the silver fir zone it does best toward the xeric end of the moisture gradient. Understories on relatively dry silver fir and mountain hemlock sites may have little vegetation growing other than beargrass and huckleberry (*Vaccinium* sp.) In Oregon's subalpine fir zone, it does best on upper south slopes and ridges. Beargrass is common in the mixed-evergreen and mixed-conifer zones on relatively cool, dry sites under Douglas-fir (*Pseudotsuga menziesii*) (Mirb.) Franco), grand fir (*Abies grandis* Douglas ex. D. Don Lindl. (Hook. Arn.), incense-cedar (*Libocedrus decurrens* Torr.), sugar pine (*Pinus lambertiana*) (Douglas), tanoak (*Lithocarpus densiflorus* (Hook Arn.) Rehder), golden chinquapin (*Chrysolepis chrysophylla* Douglas ex Hook.), and California black oak (*Quercus kelloggii* Newberry) in southern Oregon, northern California, and the Siskiyou Mountains.

Rocky Mountain continental sites—

At the northeastern limit of its range, beargrass is found on moderate to steep south-facing slopes on colluvial and morainal landforms with Engelmann spruce (*Picea engelmannii* Perry ex Engelm.), subalpine fir (*Abies lasiocarpa* (Hook) Nutt.), and whitebark pine (*Pinus albicaulis* Engelm.*)* Beargrass is dominant with menziesia (*Menziesia ferruginea* Sm.) in subalpine forests near the border between the United States and Canada. Although they grow together, beargrass favors more xeric conditions than does menziesia. In northern Idaho, beargrass grows predominantly on ridges and the upper portions of slopes. Pure stands of beargrass are found in treeless open parks with summer-dry soils on high ridges and southerly slopes in northern Idaho and eastern Washington. In northern Idaho western redcedar (*Thuja plicata* Donn ex D. Don.) stands, beargrass is most common at higher elevations. In Montana, beargrass may extend slightly from the forest into adjacent grasslands (Crane 1990). See table 3 for forest types with which beargrass is associated.

Soils—

A variety of shallow soil types, including sand, loam, sand-loam, gravel, rock, and clay-loam soils are suitable for beargrass (Crane 1990, Vance et al. 2001). Acidic soils support good beargrass growth, but growth is poor on organic, saline, or sodic soil types (Crane 1990). Soil pH within the range of beargrass ranges from 5.5. to 7.2 (USDA 2011). Crane (1990) identified granite, quartzite, serpentine, volcanic

Table 3—Forest cover types with which beargrass is associated

Forest cover types	Classification
Coastal true fir–hemlock	226
Douglas-fir–tanoak–Pacific madrone	234
Douglas-fir–western hemlock	230
Engelmann spruce–subalpine fir	206
Grand fir	213
Interior Douglas-fir	210
Lodgepole pine	218
Mountain hemlock	205
Pacific Douglas-fir	229
Port Orford-cedar	231
Red fir	207
Western larch	212
Western redcedar	228
Western redcedar–western hemlock	227
Western white pine	215
White fir	211

Source: Crane 1990.

ash, olivine gabbro, and basaltic lava as suitable for beargrass growth and limestone and pumice as not suitable. In the Northwest, beargrass is associated with soils of low fertility and productivity (e.g., serpentine soils, high in heavy metals and low in nitrogen, phosphorus, and potassium) (Peter and Shebitz 2006, Vance et al. 2001).

Beargrass tolerates a range of moisture conditions and appears to grow well on soils that are moderately to excessively well-drained. For example, it has been reported to thrive in shallow, rocky soils near ridgetops, but also inhabit forested areas with seasonally saturated soils (Higgins et al. 2004). According to Maule (1959), beargrass thrives equally well on dry sunny hillsides and on moisture-saturated soil immediately below melting snow or in bogs near sea level. It is often found on steep sites in which the soils are saturated in the spring and well drained later in the season (Crane 1990, Higgins et al. 2004, Maule 1959).

Slope—

The aspect of slope (or exposure) may be a key factor influencing the distribution and growth of beargrass. Aspect influences light availability, soil temperature, and length of the snow-free growing season. In Mount Rainier National Park, beargrass occurred most often on south-facing slopes (Maule 1959). In contrast, Brockway et al. (1983) reported that beargrass sites in the Pacific silver fir/big huckleberry and mountain hemlock/big huckleberry plant associations were the northerly aspects of upper slopes in the southern Washington Cascades.

Climatic conditions—

The annual precipitation within the range of beargrass is listed by the USDA as being from 48 to 175 cm (USDA 2011). However, Henderson et al. (1989) reported that, in high-elevation beargrass sites, mean annual precipitation has been recorded as 250 cm. Beargrass is considered very frost tolerant (Crane 1990) and is thus indicative of frost-prone environments. In particular, severe frosts can be anticipated where beargrass dominates the herbaceous layer on ridgetops, benches, and slopes less than 15 percent (Brockway et al. 1983). Beargrass has been reported to remain buried in snow until April at some California sites (Rentz 2003). It requires an average minimum of 120 frost-free days (USDA 2011).

Light environment—

The light requirements for reproduction (vegetative or sexual) and growth of beargrass are not well understood; the plant has been observed in a variety of light conditions. Beargrass can grow in dense, dark forests with little or no direct sunlight (Higgins et al. 2004) and on open slopes exposed to direct sun (Maule 1959). While the amount of light does not appear to limit beargrass survival, it may affect the reproductive strategy of this plant (see "Morphology and Reproduction" on p. 3). According to Vance et al. (2004), this species is limited by a "fairly substantial light requirement" to produce flowering stalks. The light environment affects the quantity and quality of vegetative growth (Higgins et al. 2004, Schlosser and Blatner 1997). Diffuse sunlight through an elevated forest canopy is one of the primary characteristics associated with the production of high-quality leaves for commercial harvest (Schlosser and Blatner 1997). Further information on the effects of canopy density on leaf characteristics is in the commercial harvest section, below. Overall, beargrass is reported to achieve the highest densities and reproductive success under canopy openings (i.e., dappled light environment) where it grows vigorously and blooms profusely (Crane 1990).

Ecosystem Roles

Beargrass provides food for animals large and small. Bees consume its pollen and, in spring, bears eat the fleshy part of the leaf base (Pojar and MacKinnon 1994). Likewise, mice and pocket gophers feed on the fleshy leaf bases and rhizomes (Vance et al. 2001). The flowering stalks of beargrass are eaten by a variety of mammal and insect herbivores, including elk and deer in summer, and the more tender leaves are eaten by these animals year-round (Crane 1990, Vance et al. 2001). Because the leaves remain over the winter, they also provide food for mountain

goats when resources are otherwise limited (Vance et al. 2001). Beargrass pollen provides food for a diversity of insects, including at least 36 species of flies,
beetles, and bees from at least 14 different families (Vance et al. 2004). Beargrass
leaves and flowers also provide habitat, nesting material, and foraging territory for
animals, from mice to grizzly bears (Crane 1990, Vance et al. 2004). Our focus in
this review is on pollinator insects because they have an important role in nutrient
cycling within terrestrial ecosystems and provide essential services that sustain
plant communities and form the basis of an energy-rich food web (Black et al. 2007,
Kearns et al. 1998).

Beargrass Pollination Biology

Major groups of pollinators that visit beargrass include bees (order Hymenoptera),
beetles (order Coleoptera), and flies (order Diptera). Differences exist in resource
needs, morphology, and evolutionary histories among these insect orders; summa-
ries are listed in table 4.

Pollination in every flowering plant species is restricted by several factors,
including phenology of bloom; type, quality, and quantity of rewards; floral morphology (which affects access to the rewards); and floral stimuli, such as colors,
shapes, and scents. Flower color and scent are important attractants to potential
pollinators, while nectar and pollen are important rewards (Faegri and van der Pijl
1979). Because beargrass flowers do not contain nectar, this plant is restricted to
pollinators that consume pollen as a primary reward (Vance et al. 2004) and those
that are attracted to whitish flowers with an acrid or musty scent. Despite these
limitations, beargrass attracts numerous and diverse insect pollinators (Vance et al.
2004).

Beargrass Pollination

The published, peer-reviewed literature on beargrass pollination is limited to
one study in the Oregon Cascade Range. In this study, 138 insect foragers were
observed and collected from beargrass flowers, representing members of the
Diptera (flies) Coleoptera (beetles), and Hymenoptera (bees) orders (table 5, fig. 4).
Among them, flies (91 percent of which were in the Syrphidae family) were the
most numerous and diverse group of foragers. Flower-visiting beetles (Coleoptera)
were represented by four families, of which Cermbycidae was the most common.
Four families of bees (Hymenoptera) were also collected from beargrass, although
no more than two individuals were observed from any one species (Vance et al.
2004) (table 5).

Table 4—Major beargrass pollinators groups

Pollinating group	Pollinator preferences	Pollen uses and transfer	Relative importance of group/guild	Range	Sources
Melittophily (bee pollination)	Attracted to flowers of various sizes, shapes, and colors. Pollen and nectar are important floral rewards.	Pollen is primarily gathered by adult females for larval food; nectar is consumed by male and female adults for flight fuel.	20,000 to 30,000 species worldwide of bee pollinators; most important taxon of pollinating insects. Although few bees were observed on beargrass flowers, those captured carried a large load of pollen grain.	Widespread. Bees become less active under cooler, wetter regimes, hence plants distributed at higher elevations show shifts towards fly-pollination.	Fenster et al. 2004, Kearns and Inouye 1997, O'Toole and Raw 1991
Cantharophily (beetle pollination)	Attracted to fragrant flowers, large flowers, bowl-shaped flowers with exposed sexual organs, small florets united on compact branch, open and actinomorphic flowers, white flowers. (The white-colored mass-flowering presentations of beargrass serve as favorable foraging spots for beetles.)	Adults feed on pollen, floral tissue, and nectar. Multiple beetles forage on same flower together and are coated with pollen while mating and feeding, resulting in passive transfer.	More than 184 angiosperms are pollinated almost exclusively by beetles. Not all families of beetles are pollinators. Beetles have been seen flying between multiple beargrass flowers and are therefore expected to be fairly efficient cross-pollinators.		Bernhardt 2000, Faegri and van der Pijl 1979, Gullan and Cranston 2010, Hawkeswood and Turner 2007, Kevin and Baker 1983, O'Neill et al. 2008, Young 1988
Myophily (fly pollination)	Generalists, attracted to a variety of floral scents, shapes, colors, and rewards. Hoverflies are attracted to bowl-shaped flowers with plentiful pollen and exposed sexual organs. Bee flies prefer tube-shaped flowers. Fly-pollinated flowers tend to have strong malodorous scents. (The white-colored, pollen-rich, nectarless, generally foul-smelling, mass-flowering presentations of beargrass are especially attractive to flies.)	Adults feed on pollen and nectar. Females invest lipids and amino acids from pollen into eggs. Diverse feeding, mating, and oviposition behaviors facilitate transfer of pollen.	Generally considered second most important group of pollinators. With regard to beargrass, flies are considered most effective pollinator group.	Often principal pollinators at high elevations and latitudes.	Campbell et al. 2007, Dobson, 2006, Eberling and Olesen 1999, Faegri and van der Pijl 1979, Gullan and Cranston 2010, Kearns 1992, Larson et al. 2001

Table 5—Beargrass pollinators pollen load analyses

Insect taxon	Pollen load		
	Xerophyllum tenax only	*X. tenax* and other species	No pollen
Coleopetra			
Cermbycidae			
Anastrangalia laetifica	2	1	0
Cosmosalia chrysacoma	18	7	0
Leptaura proponqua	1	0	0
Cleridae			
Trichodes orantus	2	3	0
Meloidae			
Epicauta sp.	12	0	1
Scarabaeidae			
Dichelonyx backi	2	0	0
Diploytaxis sp.	1	0	0
Subtotals	38	11	1
Diptera			
Acroceridae			
Eulonchus sp.	1	0	0
Asilidae			
Laphria sp.	0	0	1
Bombyllidae			
Conphorus sp.	1	0	0
Calliphoridae			
Calliphora vomitoria	1	0	0
Tachinidae			
Tachina sp.	0	1	0
Syrphidae			
Cheilosia hoodiana	20	0	1
Chrysotoxum fasciantum	4	0	1
Eriozona laxa	3	0	0
Eupeodes abberrantis	1	0	0
Hardromyia crawfordi	1	0	0
Hardromyia pulcher	1	0	0
Melangya triangulifera	1	0	0
Parasyrphus relictus	18	1	0
Sericomyia chalopyga	1	0	0
Syritta pipiens	1	0	0
Syrphus opinator	5	1	0
Syphus ribesii	3	2	0
Subtotals	61	5	3
Hymenoptera			
Andrenidae			
Andrenidie nivalis	0	1	0
Andrenidie vicina	1	1	0

Table 5—Beargrass pollinators pollen load analyses (continued)

Insect taxon	Pollen load		
	Xerophyllum tenax only	*X. tenax* and other species	No pollen
Apidae			
Apis mellifera	1	0	0
Bombus fernaldi	0	1	0
Halitidae			
Halictus rubicundus sp.	0	1	0
Lasioglossum athabascence	1	1	0
Lasigolossum sp. 1 *(Dialictus)*	1	0	0
Lasigolossum sp. 2 *(Dialictus)*	2	0	0
Lasigolossum sp. *(Evylaceus)*	1	1	0
Megacgulidae			
Coelioxys sp.	1	0	0
Megachile vidua	0	1	0
Subtotals	8	6	0
Grand totals	110	23	5

Source: Vance et al. 2004.

Figure 4—Insects from several orders have been documented as pollinators of beargrass.

Beargrass pollinators exhibited notable differences in sex ratios between insect groups, which potentially reflect differences in resource needs and sexual function between insect groups (Vance et al. 2004). More than 62 percent of the hover flies were female, perhaps because they were attracted to the abundance of pollen produced by beargrass to use lipids and amino acids to invest in eggs. In contrast, male hover flies, not in need of pollen for egg production, may be less attracted to the nectarless flowers of beargrass (Vance et al. 2004). The majority of collected bees were female, like flies. As male bees are generally short lived, lower in overall abundance, and not tasked with collecting pollen for any offspring (and therefore not, theoretically, attracted to the nectarless flowers of beargrass), this result is not surprising. Unlike flies and bees, the male-to-female sex ratio of beetles was relatively high—64 percent of the 50 beetle specimens examined were male, including 92 percent of the common *Cosmosalia chrysocoma* (23 of 25 specimens). The high ratio of male beetles on beargrass inflorescences is likely owing to a previously documented beetle courtship behavior in which a male waits for the arrival of unfertilized beetles on preferred flowers (Bernhardt 2000, Vance et al. 2004).

Direct observation of insect behavior and analyses of the pollen load carried by insects found on beargrass flowers suggest that flies, beetles, and bees do not contribute equally to the cross-pollination of beargrass (Vance et al. 2004). Based on visitation frequency and pollen load, Vance et al. (2004) identified hover flies as the most "faithful" vectors of beargrass pollen, likely to be affecting the majority of cross-pollination. Beetles appeared to be less efficient but still effective pollinators. Bees, in general, were the least frequently observed of all insect visitors. Their low abundance does not necessarily translate to insignificance, however. The bees that were observed and analyzed were found to carry the highest number of pollen grains, which may counterbalance their lower observed frequency. Bees are generally recognized for their ability to work flowers at a much greater speed than other visitors and therefore are likely to contribute more to pollination than is indicated by their frequency alone (Fenster et al. 2004).

Life History Patterns of Main Pollinating Species/Guilds

A basic understanding of life history patterns of the major beargrass pollinator groups and species can help in making decisions about management activities that support ecosystem diversity and species conservation. Ranges of key pollinators may also be informative in determining potential regional effects of management strategies on pollinators, as well as in assessing the potential for discovering new pollinators in unstudied regions. Life history patterns (including feeding behavior, mating, and life cycle) and ranges (including preferred habitats) of key beargrass pollinators are presented in table 6. The responses of these species and groups to disturbances are discussed further in the disturbance section of this review.

Importance of Pollinators to Beargrass

Mutualistic relationships between plants and pollinators date to the Cretaceous period, when insects began to acquire food from flowers and flowers achieved higher reproductive success through the movement of pollen by insects (Kearns and Inouye 1997). At present, the majority of flowering plants utilize insects for pollination (Kremen et al. 2007, Tepedino 1979) although dependence on insect pollination differs by plant species (Kearns and Inouye 1997). Beargrass may rely on insects to spread its pollen because the plant is self-incompatible (Vance et al. 2004). This means the stigmatic ridge recognizes and rejects pollen produced by the same plant (Sage et al. 2000). Although it is mechanically possible for beargrass to self-pollinate, Vance et al. (2004) reported that resulting fruits had a lower rate of filled seed. Self-incompatibility has also been noted for trillium, which—like beargrass—is a member of the Melanthiaceae.

Vance et al. (2004) found that the effectiveness of an insect's cross-pollination service is compromised by the tendency of some insect pollinators to visit more than one flower on the same inflorescence. This results in the transfer of incompatible pollen grains. Beargrass is, therefore, considered to be "compatible-pollen limited," as even in open-pollinated flowers, seed set remains relatively low, despite the fact that this species produces large quantities of pollen and attracts many insect pollinators (Vance et al. 2004). Still, cross-pollination by insects enables transport of beargrass pollen between compatible genets and results in significantly higher fitness than self-pollination.

Potential effects of changes in pollinator communities on beargrass—
A growing body of evidence suggests that both managed honey bee colonies and wild pollinators are experiencing significant declines (Black et al. 2007). The causes of decline are difficult to pinpoint, but loss of floral diversity and habitat from urbanization and land use change, expansion of intensive agriculture, invasive plants, pesticide use, climate change, disease, and parasites are all believed to have negative effects on pollinator populations (National Research Council 2006). Pollinator decline can affect plants in several ways, including reduction of viable seeds, which limits sexual reproductive success (Kearns and Inouye 1997) and production of less vigorous offspring, because in the absence of pollinators, a higher percentage of seeds may be set through self-pollination. In beargrass, self-pollination is known to be an inferior mating system (Vance et al. 2004). Within an

Table 6—Life history of main species/guilds of beargrass pollinators

Classification	Diet/feeding behavior	Mating/life-cycle	Range/habitat	Sources
Order: Diptera Major family: Syrphidae (hover flies) Representative species: Cheilosia hoodiana Parasyrphus relictus Syrphus opinator Syrphus ribesii	Larval diet varies widely in the syrphid family. The larvae of *Cheilosia hoodiana* feed on living fir trees in the Northwest. Very little material has been published on the life history of *Parasyrphus relictus*. The larvae are likely predaceous. Adult syrphid flies feed chiefly on pollen, which they require for ovary development and possibly sperm production. Most syrphids have short proboscises, which they use to probe the stamens and style arms of flowers while foraging. These flies move rapidly between flowers, facilitating a quick spread of pollen. Although syrphids frequent multiple plants for foraging, they have been observed to exhibit preferences for certain flowering plant species when multiple species are in flower. With regard to beargrass, a pollination study suggests some syrphid species may exhibit a strong preference (possible seasonal dependence) for beargrass pollen.	The life-cycle of *Cheilosia hoodiana*, a major beargrass pollinator, is probably similar to that of the related hemlock bark maggot (*Cheilosia burkei*) which has been studied in greater detail. Adults lay eggs in springtime in resin-filled tree wounds. The hatched maggots enter the bark through the wound and feed on sap and soft tissues, utilizing a long, telescopic, protractile tail that extends through the resin for breathing. Larval feeding continues for up to five years, followed by springtime pupation (7 days) in resin at the entrance of the wound. Wasp parasitism is not uncommon in syrphids—the larval stage of *C. hoodiana* is parasitized by the ichneumonid wasp, *Syrphoctonus maculifron*.	*Cheilosia hoodiana* occurs along the Pacific coast, including California and Oregon, and eastward to New Mexico. The distribution of *Parasypha relictus* is not readily available. In addition to beargrass, this species has been recorded on flowers of *Cornus canadensis* (Cornaceae), *Clintonia borealis* (Liliaceae), and *Maianthemum canadense* (Liliaceae).	Barrett and Helenurm 1987, Burke 1905, Campbell et al. 2007, Cole 1969, Drabble and Drabble 1917, F.S. doc n.d., Gullan and Cranston 2010, Larson et al. 2001, McGehey 1967, Owen and Gilbert 1989, Rank and Smiley 1994, Robertson 1929, Vance et al. 2004, Weems 1954, Wheeler 1908.
Order: Coleoptera Major family: Cerambycidae (long-horn beetles) Representative species: Anastrangalia laetifica Cosmosalia chrysocoma	Larvae of *C. chrysocoma* feed on decaying wood and have been successfully reared on the coniferous *Pinus ponderosa* and *P. flexilis*, as well as some hardwoods. Cerambycidae adults are relatively strong fliers that actively seek out flowers and feed primarily on pollen. Beetles move among neighboring inflorescences, coating themselves in pollen dust. *C. chrysocoma* adults are known to congregate on flowering plants in subalpine lodgepole pine habitat, and have been observed on the same beargrass inflorescence for over an hour.	Larval feeding results in extensive, frass-filled galleries or tunnels under the bark or within the sapwood of the host tree. Most western species feed first in the cambium region of their hosts, then extend their tunnels into the sapwood. Tunnels terminate in a pupal chamber near the bark, where metamorphosis from last-instar larva to pupa to adult takes place. Life spans of temperate Cerambycidae species range from one to three years, most of which is spent in the larval stage. Adults emerge disperse,, reproduce, and die within a few days to a few months. Courtship and mating frequently takes place on flowers and foliage of adult food plants. Eggs are laid singly in natural cracks in the host bark or in shallow pits chewed by the female.	*C. chrysocoma* distribution covers much of the United States and Canada, from the West to the Northeast and south to Northern Mexico, including Oregon, Washington, Montana, Idaho, and California. Adults fly from June to at least August in the Rocky Mountains and Pacific Coast Range. In addition to the role of adults as pollinators, cerambycid larvae provide a vital "first step" in the decomposition and bio-recycling of wood in forest ecosystems. Cerambycid beetles may also be valuable bio-indicators of forest health and diversity.	Craighead 1923, Goldsmith 1987, Hagle et al. 2003, MacRae and Rice 2007, Monne and Bezark 2010, Makino et al. 2007 O'Neill et al. 2008, Sutherland 2006, Vance et al. 2004, Yanega 1996.

Table 6—Life history of main species/guilds of beargrass pollinators (continued)

Classification	Diet/feeding behavior	Mating/life-cycle	Range/habitat	Sources
Order: Coleoptera Major family: Meloidae (blister beetles) Representative species: *Epicauta* sp.	Adults are herbivorous on an array of angiosperms and are strongly attracted to blooming food plants. In addition to feeding, courtship and mating activities generally occur on flowering plants. Although some species may be significant "mess and soil" pollinators, their potential to impede pollination via other pollinators must also be considered. The consequences of floral herbivory, therefore, may outweigh the benefits of *Epicauta* pollination.	Most blister beetles have one generation per year. Adults lay egg clusters in the soil; upon hatching the long-legged, first-instar larvae actively seek out and prey upon the egg pods of subterranean grasshoppers (Acridoidea), including many crop-damaging species. The larvae pass through numerous grub-like, phases—the first four larval stages develop within about month, but the second to the last (pseudopupa) can remain for about 230 days before molting into the final (sixth) larval stage. Overwintering takes place in the psuedopupal stage, with the final stage occurring in the spring. Pupation, which generally lasts for about 2 weeks, occurs in late spring, and adults emerge from the soil in early summer. Adult activity period occurs May through September, although peaks vary by species.	*Epicauta* is the largest genus of blister beetles in North America, with 173 species north of Mexico and a wide distribution across the continent and globe.	Arnett et al. 2002, Bernhardt and Thien 1986, Capinera 2008, Cardel and Kopter 2010, Drees and Jackman 1999, Haddock and Chaplin 1982, Kerr and Packer 1999, Kinney et al. 2010, McLain 1982.
Order: Apoidea (bees) Major families: Andrenidae Apidae Halactidae Magachilidae	All bee species are dependent on flowers for meeting larval and adult nutritional needs. Foraging bees may be categorized as specialists or generalists—highly-specialist patterns are rare, but occasionally exhibited by species of solitary Andrenidae and Megachilidae bees. The majority of bees (including Andrenidae, Megachilidae, and Halictidae) perform "mass-provisioning," in which egg cells are provisioned with food (pollen) for larvae to eat upon hatching. Apidae perform "progressive provisioning," in which larvae are fed pollen repeatedly as they develop. One theory suggests the light colors, disagreeable odors, and nectarless condi-tion of beargrass flowers are unattractive to the majority of bees. The few bees observed were generally seen scraping or vibrating t he anthers of beargrass flowers for pollen while the ventral portions of their b bodies ounced against the style arms.	Bees are a diverse group with a variety of habitat specializations and life history strategies. Bees range from solitary to eusocial. Mating behavior frequently involves specific pheromones b that ring the two sexes together. In many, species males emerge before females and wait for the females. The male lifespan is relatively short; males can often only be found at the beginning of a species' season.	Bees nest in a variety of habitats, including living and dead wood, sandstone, and soil. They may utilize existing hollows (such as rodent burrows), or construct their own nests of soil or plant material. Although solitary bees build their nests individually, numerous nests of the same ground-nesting species are often found together in a small area of suitable habitat.	Matheson et al. 1996, Moretti et al. 2009, Pendleton et al. 2008, Ramel 1995, Roulston et al. 2000, Vance et al. 2008.

ecosystem, reduced seed and fruit production owing to declines in plant-pollinator mutualism can have cascading effects, particularly for organisms that consume or otherwise rely on the seeds, fruits, or vegetation of insect-pollinated plants (Kearns and Inouye 1997).

Beargrass appears to have multiple compensation mechanisms to ensure survival and reproduction in reduced-pollinator environments and may be classified as intermediate in its overall potential for fitness-loss resulting from pollinator declines. The effect of pollinator decline on any particular plant species requires understanding several factors including lifespan, potential for vegetative reproduction, characteristics of the existing seed bank, and whether the pollination relationship is generalist or specialist and facultative or obligate (Kearns and Inouye 1997). Plant species most at risk from loss of a pollinator are those that propagate only by seeds, have a single pollinator (specialist pollination), and are self-incompatible (obligate pollination). Beargrass only partially fits this risk profile. Rather, it is a long-lived plant capable of vegetative reproduction via offshoots of the rhizome and is visited by several species of insect pollinators. Although the relationship between beargrass and its pollinators is generalistic (multiple species perform pollination services in the flowers), it is also obligate (insect pollination is critical owing to fitness reductions in self-pollinated flowers).

If a population of beargrass remains intact, plants within it can likely maintain their genetic structure through rhizomatous regeneration and growth, even when environmental conditions do not favor flowering or pollination (Vance et al. 2004). However, if a population is reduced in number by disturbances that displace entire plants, outcrossing by sexual reproduction may be necessary to achieve sufficient gene flow and remixing of alleles for demographic recovery of the population (Collins and Fore 2009, Vance et al. 2004). The seed bank characteristics of beargrass are not well understood, but the potential seed production for a given plant ranges from approximately 350 to 2,800 seeds, based on reports of 40 to 500 flowers per plant (Munger 2003, Vance et al. 2001) and an average of 7 seeds per capsule (Vance et al. 2004). Soil seed banks can buffer plants from local extinction when an important pollinator declines (Kearns and Inouye 1997), but the persistence and viability of beargrass seed is unknown.

Importance of Beargrass to Pollinators

Beargrass is an important food resource to a diverse assemblage of insects (Vance et al. (2004); however, the comparative importance of beargrass relative to other plants frequented by the same insect is unknown. Pollen provides most of the dietary nitrogen for most bee species and many species of beetles and other insects

(Roulston et al. 2000). Increased consumption of pollen protein and other nutrients may increase the size, survival, longevity, and fecundity of bees, flies, and other pollinating insects (Roulston et al. 2000, Vance et al. 2004). In one analysis of the pollen load from insect foragers collected on beargrass flowers, 80 percent of the insects carried beargrass pollen exclusively, which suggests that they had a seasonal dependence or preference for beargrass pollen (Vance et al. 2004) (table 5). Insects carrying mixed pollen loads had a maximum of two extra pollen types in addition to beargrass. All of the additional pollen grains came from common coflowering associates of beargrass in the Western Cascades (Vance et al. 2004) and may compete with beargrass for the limited pollinator guild. However, beargrass is nectarless (Vance et al. 2004) and most pollen consumers seek nectar as well as pollen (Roulston et al. 2000). On one occasion, a blister beetle (*Epicauta* sp.) was observed flying from beargrass to flowers of another plant (*Ceanothus velutinus* Douglas ex Hook.) to drink nectar (Vance et al. 2004).

The specific nutritional information of beargrass pollen has not been examined. Angiosperm pollen is generally a nutrient-rich resource, containing protein, sugar, starch, fat, and trace amounts of vitamins and organic salts (Gullan and Cranston 2010). However, the nutritional value of pollen differs among plant species. This variability means that, although another member of the Liliales order have been reported to have pollen composed of 17.1 percent protein, this may not be true for beargrass (Roulston et al. 2000). The abundance and nutritional value of beargrass pollen may change under different environmental conditions, as has been shown in greenhouse studies of zucchini (*Cucurbito pepo* L.) (Lau and Stephenson 1993, 1994). Soil phosphorus and nitrogen levels in those studies were both found to have had significant effects on pollen production per flower and size of pollen grains produced (Lau and Stephenson 1993, 1994).

Tribal and Contemporary Uses and Values for Beargrass

In addition to its ecological role, and its importance to pollinators, beargrass is valued and used by people. The role of beargrass in human cultures encompasses secular and sacred needs, personal and commercial uses, and community and environmental purposes.

Native American Uses and Values

Beargrass is valued by Native Americans for use in basketry and regalia (fig. 5.); as an edible delicacy; for medicinal, cosmetic, and decorative purposes; and for

Doug Hill

Figure 5 —Large berry harvesting basket made by Nettie Jackson in the traditional Klickitat style. Photo courtesy of Maryhill Museum of Art, Goldendale, Washington.

spiritual, ceremonial, and aesthetic reasons (fig. 6). **Beargrass leaves are durable, yet flexible, and can be worked into tight weaves that are** ideal for the creation of baskets (Turner 1998) (fig. 7). Additionally, Klamath Mountain tribes (Karok, Hupa, and Yurok) wrap and interweave leaf blades to make "braids," which serve as long slender "beads" on women's dress fringe and necklaces, and on men's quivers and dance aprons (fig. 8). Older, thicker leaves are used as stuffing or filler in men's regalia in headrolls, and wrapped in buckskin leather (Heffner 1984). This report focuses primarily on the uses and value of beargrass within traditional basketry, which constitutes the majority of native uses for the plant.

Cultural Value of Basketry

The value of basketry is not restricted to the utilitarian function of a particular object. In Native American culture, basketry is also "a sacred practice that is important to maintaining the role of certain entities in our lives and recording our history" (CHiXapkaid, quoted in Shebitz 2005). Baskets are "symbols of identity"

Figure 6—Basket cap created by an unknown Yurok weaver using beargrass as the white overlay material.

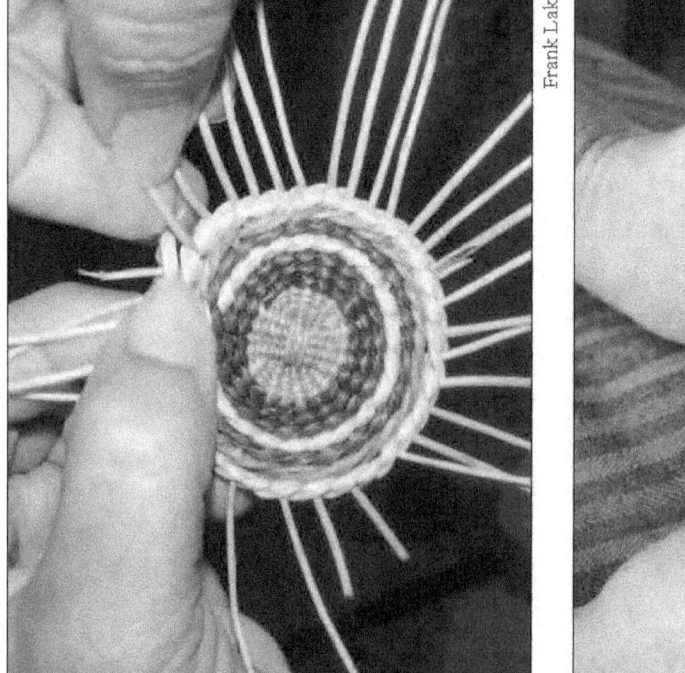

Figure 7—Basket weaving demonstration by Deanna Marshall using beargrass.

Frank Lake

Figure 8—Braids of beargrass made by Frank Lake. Other materials include grey pine nuts with abalone beads strung on leather.

for the families and tribes that weave them (Brotherton 2008). The symbology of a particular basket showcases the skill of an individual weaver (Lobb 1990), and also is a portrait of a tribe's history and mythology (Shebitz 2005). The art of basketry is therefore "a community resource" (Jones 1983) as the basket is a medium through which identity and knowledge can be passed from generation to generation (Marr 2008, Shebitz and Kimmerer 2005). Basketry is often "a family tradition—one that crosses borders, reaching into many communities. Designs and techniques travel with people as they move between communities." Baskets are therefore "more than just containers for food, tools, and other types of belongings; they contain and carry forward memories and identities about who we are as people... [Baskets] carry everyday reminders of our grandparents and ancestors, their spiritual gifts and individual creativity" (Fortney 2008).

Native Americans in California and the Pacific Northwest have experienced significant changes in their cultures and lifestyles over the past century; nonetheless, basketry continues to be an integral part of their culture and traditions (Rentz

2003, Shebitz 2005). "The act of creating a basket unites the maker with his or her culture, continuing a tradition that has been passed on from countless generations" (Marr 2008). Harvesting and treating beargrass for use in basketry strengthens and maintains cultures by preserving knowledge and traditions (Shebitz and Kimmerer 2005). The tending and harvesting of beargrass also intimately connects tribal people to the forested ecosystems in which beargrass grows. "Today, each tribe's use of particular plant materials marks its distinctive culture and plays a major role in shaping, defining, and maintaining its cultural identity…The continuation of gathering and hunting traditions is an important component of tribal identity and preservation of culture" (Anderson 2005). Although today the number of basket makers has declined and the practices of those that remain have changed, weavers still "represent an art form with ancient roots, one that has survived decades of social change… [Contemporary basket makers] may change some of the new materials, they may create new designs or change the shapes of their baskets, but they nevertheless remain closely connected to the masters" (Marr 2008).

Basketry also has sociocultural value to non-Native society. Old baskets give contemporary researchers and anthropologists information on changing cultural practices and values, and on changing ecological conditions (Brotherton 2008, Shebitz 2005). Baskets are products of specific places and distinct times, and social scientists are able to better understand those places and periods in history by observing changes over time in a basket's function, form, and construction. The materials used to create a particular basket can help inform ecologists about species availability, growth, and condition when the basket was created; changes in the materials used might indicate changing ecological conditions, or suggest trade with another tribe (Shebitz 2005).

Native American Harvesters

Beargrass was harvested by many tribes in northern California, up the Pacific Coast, onto the Olympic Peninsula, and into southeastern British Columbia (Anderson 2005, O'Neale 1932, Turner 1998). Tribes as diverse as the Modoc, the Yurok, the Maidu, and the Shasta gathered young, fresh beargrass "tillers" (Anderson 2005). The Nuu-chah-nulth and Coast Salish of Vancouver Island used this grass, as did the Squamish, Sechelt, Nlaka'pamux, Okanagan, and Ktunaxa (Brotherton 2008, Turner 1998). Some groups had direct access to the plant; others obtained it through trade. A study of Yurok-Karuk basketry in northern California conducted by O'Neale (1932) found that, in 1928, basket makers would pay as much as 50 cents a bushel for beargrass leaves. In the mid 20th century, a small bundle of prepared beargrass leaves cost about 50 cents (Turner 1998). In the same region

(Heffner 1984), materials at the Northern California Indian Development Council's Art Center in Eureka, California, were sold listed as "Plant, Bear Grass; Amount, 3; diameter/bunch; Cost, $5.00."

Seasonality and Location of Native American Harvest

Beargrass is harvested primarily during spring and summer, after snowmelt, with special focus given to areas that have burned sometime over the last 1 to 3 years (Crane 1990, Hunter 1988, O'Neale 1930, Rentz 2003, Schlick 1994, Shebitz 2005, Shebitz et al. 2009a, Vance et al. 2001). High-elevation plants produce longer and stronger (less brittle) leaves (Hunter 1988, Rentz 2003), and beargrass plants beneath a partial canopy, or in partial shade, produce leaves that are less bleached and that remain pliable for a longer period of time (Anderson 2005, Hunter 1988, Shebitz 2005, Thomas and Schumann 1993). Leaves on an open slope are believed to curl, yellow, and become more brittle in the sunlight (Anderson 2005, O'Neale 1930, Rentz 2003, Schlick 1994).

Native Americans used fire to prepare beargrass habitat, probably because exposure to low-intensity fire increased leaf quality (Hunter 1988, LaLande and Pullen 1999, O'Neale 1930, Shebitz 2005). Researchers have documented that leaves harvested from recently burned sites are less pigmented, thinner, and stronger (Hunter 1988, Rentz 2003). Rentz (2003) found that beargrass collected from burned areas exhibited reductions in support fibers along the adaxial and abaxial surfaces, making the leaves more pliable. Crane (1990) found that leaves can be harvested from a burned site within a year after a fire, but Anderson (2005), Shebitz et al. (2009a), LaLande and Pullen (1999) and Rentz (2003) all noted that the best harvest is 3 to 7 years following a burn, with the timing likely related to fire severity. Today, anthropogenic burning by Native Americans for the management of cultural resources is limited (see Senos et al. 2006: 394, fig. 17.1—Hoopa Forestry), and, therefore, most beargrass is harvested following a wildfire (Heffner 1984). In one unreplicated field study, Shebitz et al. (2009a) found that high-intensity rather than the mid-to-low-intensity fire better prepared the site for beargrass establishment.

Many Native American beargrass harvesters are now elderly; therefore, site accessibility is also an important consideration, and sites adjacent to maintained roads are often preferred (Hunter 1988). Harvest occurs on public and private lands, as well as on reservation lands. Reservations were often created great distances from traditional gathering sites, so foraging on public lands remains common despite the greater distances that must be traveled to reach a suitable harvesting area (Heffner 1984, Lobb 1990, Lynch and McLain 2003). Most landowners, public and private, allow cultural harvesters to harvest for a nominal fee, or for free, based on a case-by-case evaluation (Hansis 1998, Lynch and McLain 2003).

Traditional Harvest Practices

Weavers favor longer, thinner, more pliable leaves with less pigmentation, and a snowy white color at the base (fig. 9). Brittle leaves or leaves with a yellowish tint are not suitable for weaving (Crane 1990, Hunter 1988, LaLande and Pullen 1999, Rentz 2003, Schlick 1994, Shebitz 2005, Shebitz et al. 2009a, Thomas and Schumann 1993). Additionally, older larger, thicker leaves with the red-tinged leaf edges near base are avoided. Leaves must be flexible enough to work with, and lay flat in the design, but be strong enough to withstand the stress of weaving (Rentz 2003). Harvesters select only the longest blades from the center of the plant (Anderson 2005), which are gently pulled or cut at the base. Leaves are cut when the plant has reached full maturity, so the root systems are not damaged in harvesting, and the plant can grow the following year (Anderson 2005, Turner and Peacock 2005). One good plant will provide enough leaves to cover a gallon-size basket (Schlick 1994). A weaver might use as many as 2,000 leaves to complete a large basket (Rentz 2003). This harvesting practice may also prevent subsequent flowering by leaving tillers, but empirical evidence is lacking.

To make beargrass leaves (or "blades") more flexible for weaving, a weaver first removes the spine on the underside of the blade with a fingernail or a sharp knife (Anderson 2005, Schlick 1994). A weaver will then twist the blades lengthwise (taking care not to cut their hands as the edges of the leaf are razor sharp) to keep them soft and pliable and lay them out to cure in the sunlight for 1 to 3 days (Anderson 2005, O'Neale 1930, Schlick 1994). When exposed to sunlight, blades fade to a lighter whitish color, Too much sun exposure can result in a yellow, brittle blade, which is undesirable. Once the leaves are cured and sun-bleached, weavers split them to the desired width and sort them into 4 to 5 sizes before braiding them together for storage (Anderson 2005, O'Neale 1930, Storm 1985). Blades can also be dyed—either with natural materials like wolf lichen (*Letharia* sp.) or Oregon grape (*Berberis aquifolium* Pursh.) (Anderson 2005, O'Neale 1930), or with synthetic materials like Kool-Aid® (Turner 1998).

Commercial Value of Basketry

Over time, tribes developed specialized basketry styles and techniques that were not widely shared (Brotherton 2008, Lobb 1990). The Klickitat, a tribe in the Columbia River basin, developed a style of coiled cedar root basketry, embellished with beargrass, that was particularly valued (Hunn 1990). Such specialization created an informal industry between tribes. Strategic marriages helped facilitate the trade of more nuanced basketry techniques (Brotherton 2008). Seasonal work opportunities brought families from distant communities together, and further

Figure 9—Beargrass leaves harvested (top), sorted, and bundled by size (bottom) after being sun-dried.

facilitated intertribal trade in basketry (Gunther 1927). Thrush (2007) related that basket vendors in Seattle during this time were not necessarily from Puget Sound but came from as far away as Vancouver Island, suggesting that trade in basketry was an important source of income for native people. In California, O'Neale reported a similar demand. Baskets produced by the Yurok and Karuk tribes sold for as much as $35 in 1928 (O'Neale 1930).

Basketry can still be an important source of income to a contemporary weaver (Shebitz and Kimmerer 2005). Depending on size, intricacy, and overall quality, an individual basket can fetch between $65 and $3,500 (Thomas and Schumann 1993). However, one tribe member reported that his wife only made $5,000 within a 12-month period (Thomas and Schumann 1993) owing to the time and difficulty it took to gather supplies and weave the actual baskets.

The Commercial Floral Greens Industry

Floral greens, as a group, are the stems, branches and leaves of plants that are used in floral arrangements. Floral greens contribute as much as $8 billion to the global economy (Draffan 2006). Greens commonly harvested from the Pacific Northwest and British Columbia include salal (*Gaultheria* L. sp.), evergreen huckleberry (*Gaylussacia* K. sp.), beargrass, assorted mosses and ferns, and boughs of Douglas-fir, noble fir (*Abies procera* Donn ex D. Don (Douglas ex D. Don) Lindl), white pine (*Pinus monticola* Douglas ex D. Don), western red cedar (*Thuja plicata*), and Port Orford cedar (*Chamaecyparis lawsoniana* (A. Murray bis.) Parl) (McLain and Lynch 2010). Beargrass did not enter the floral green industry in commercial quantities until the late 1980s (Lynch and McLain 2003, Weigand 2002). The leaves are used as floral arrangements (Blatner and Alexander 1998, Schlosser and Blatner 1998, Thomas and Schuman 1993). Beargrass leaves are popular in part because, when fresh, their vibrant green color is attractive (Schlosser et al. 1992, Thomas and Schuman 1997) and when dried they are easily dyed (Thomas and Schuman 1993, Turner 1998).

Commercial harvest occurs in the Pacific Northwest and British Columbia, and extends into Idaho and northern California. Most processing is done in the south-eastern portion of the Olympic Peninsula in the state of Washington (McLain and Lynch 2010). In 1987, reports suggested that beargrass was the most harvested species in the floral greens industry of the Pacific Northwest (Schlosser et al. 1992). Sheds might purchase materials harvested from as far away as 1609 km (Schlosser et al. 1991). Elsewhere in the range of the plant, between 1999 and 2001, 200 488 kg (442,000 pounds) of beargrass were harvested from the Idaho Panhandle National Forests (Kramer 2001). In 1997, beargrass was established as the most widely harvested floral green species in the Pacific Northwest (Schlosser and Blatner 1997).

Research suggests that as agricultural jobs disappear, the harvest of forest products like beargrass becomes increasingly important to local economies, especially workers who depend on natural resources for a livelihood (Brown 2001, 1998, Hansis 1996). Little information exists detailing the history and evolution of beargrass harvesting (as an isolated species) within the floral greens industry. This section therefore discusses the floral greens industry as a whole.

Market Stakeholders

Stakeholders in the floral greens industry include harvesters, buyers who purchase harvested materials, owners of land from which beargrass is harvested, wholesalers that distribute materials to retailers, and consumers (table 7).

Until 1970, the floral greens industry of the Pacific Northwest included a handful of large wholesale companies and numerous independent buying sheds. The workforce was made up of rural, seasonally self-employed U.S. citizens, or recent Euro-American immigrants (McLain and Lynch 2010). Ethnic composition of the workforce changed in the 1980s when two of the larger wholesalers of floral greens in the region, facing a shortage of locally available labor, brought in crews of Latino agricultural migrant workers (table 8). Rather than returning to agricultural work, many Latino workers chose to stay in the Pacific Northwest harvesting floral greens (Hansis 1996, 1998; McLain and Lynch 2010; Schlosser and Blatner 1997).

A federal law also discouraged employers in related industries from using undocumented workers (McLain and Lynch 2010), thereby increasing the reliance of these workers on informal economies like floral greens. By 1990, 80 to 80 percent of floral greens harvested from the Pacific Northwest were being shipped to Europe (McLain and Lynch 2010, Schlosser and Blatner 1997, Schlosser et al. 1991, Thomas and Schumann 1993, Vance et al. 2001). At the same time, Southeast Asian refugees arriving in the Pacific Northwest from Cambodia, Laos, and Vietnam began harvesting floral greens (including beargrass), as it was one of the only viable and available ways to earn a living (Hansis 1996).

European consumption still fuels beargrass harvesting in the Pacific Northwest. Thomas and Schumann (1993) found that a U.S. company that sold one or two 9.1 kg (20 pound) boxes of beargrass per week to U.S. buyers could sell up to a thousand boxes a week to Europe.

Harvesting Practices

Beargrass of commercial harvest quality is deep green and has long, wide, and firm leaves. Leaves that are too short or have yellowing tips are unacceptable (Schlosser et al. 1992, Schlosser and Blatner 1997, Thomas and Schumann 1993). Research suggests that the highest quality (darker and longer) leaves are located in the center

Table 7—Characteristics of the labor force in the commercial market for beargrass

	Size of labor force	Ethnic composition	Source
Harvesters	In 1989, there were an estimated 2,670 full time, and 2,750 part time, harvesters in the floral greens industry within the Pacific Northwest. [The literature does not have more recent estimates.]	In the late 1980s/early 1990s, the workforce was primarily made up of people of Southeast Asian heritage. Latino workers began entering the market in the early to mid 1990s, dominating the workforce by 2003. Common ethnicities include Mexican, Honduran, Cambodian, Hmong, Vietnamese, Laotian, Thai, Korean, and Guatemalan very few White harvesters have been reported.	Hansis 1996, 1998; Lynch and McLain, 2003; Schlosser et al 1991; Thomas and Schumann 1993
Buyers	In 1993 there were a dozen buyers (either small companies or individuals) located in Washington state and purchasing beargrass on a regular basis. It is estimated the buyer's industry in the Pacific Northwest to be 60 small businesses, concentrated in Washington, supporting a total of 700 full time and 4,180 seasonal workers.	Small companies in the buyers industry are usually owned by White Americans. Owners increasingly hire Latina women to staff the establishment and sort, clean, preserve, and box incoming material.	Brown 2001 Lynch and McLain 2003, Schlosser et al. 1991, Schlosser and Blatner 1997, Thomas and Schumann 1993

Table 8—Demographics and characteristics of commercial beargrass harvesters

All harvesters	Source
Self employed.	
Use multipronged income strategy, harvesting to supplement wages or fill gaps in employment. Split between part-time and full-time, although part-time is on the rise.	Brown 2001; Lynch and McLain 2003; Hansis 1996, 1998; Schlosser and Blatner1997; Schlosser et al. 1991
Constitute an invisible workforce, as they are often undocumented, have few legal rights, and may not speak English. Usually resist making contact with land managers or researchers, and are hesitant to provide personal information for fear of restricted access or deportation.	
May be fleeing harsh conditions elsewhere that lead them to work cheaply and under poor labor conditions.	

Latino	East Asian harvesters	Source
Younger, more mobile, more often males, typically harvest as individuals, willing to take risks.	Harvest in family groups and are more stable, tend to be more integrated into society. Individuals often obtain permits, and act as crew leaders to Latino or non-English-speaking harvesters unable to navigate the system, often charging for the service. Individuals often own vans and charge exorbitant fees to other harvesters for transportation to the forest, or transportation of harvested material to buying sheds.	Brown 2001, Hansis 1996, 1998; McLain 2003

of a plant (Thomas and Schumann 1993). Leaf quality is maximized during later stages of mid-successional development (Schlosser and Blatner 1997). Generally, only older, larger plants bear leaves that are long enough to harvest (Thomas and Schumann 1993).

Commercial harvesters are able to collect beargrass leaves year-round for the floral greens industry (Crane 1990, Schlosser et al. 1992, Thomas and Schumann 1993), but generally prefer spring and summer (Hansis 1996, 1998; Lynch and McLain 2003; Schlosser and Blatner 1997). Commercial harvest can occur legally on public lands (managed by the USDA Forest Service, USDI Bureau of Land Management, or the states) and on private forest lands (Lynch and McLain 2003). In 1991, 8 percent of harvested material on the Olympic Peninsula came from producer-owned lands (Schlosser et al. 1991). Harvest is illegal in national parks.

Several factors influence demand for beargrass. Demand tends to increase around holidays (McLain and Lynch 2010), but there can be rapid unanticipated changes in tastes and preferences, which can affect demand (Blatner and Alexander 1998). The availability and relative value of new harvestable material (Blatner and Alexander 1998) and decline of other forms of employment may also affect the demand for beargrass expressed by buying sheds (Hansis 2002, Lynch and McClain 2003).

Permitting and Regulation

Prior to the 1950s, landowners often allowed harvesters to collect floral greens from their land (McLain and Lynch 2010). Throughout the 1980s, as the number of harvesters increased, landowners began to formalize access to floral greens. Multiple forms of permitting resulted, many of which are still used. The Fiscal Year 2000 Appropriations Act required the Forest Service to charge a fair market value for nontimber forest product permits, and to monitor harvesting levels to ensure that the harvest of nontimber forest products on Forest Service lands was sustainable and affordable (Lynch and McLain 2003). Many harvesters may be able to afford inexpensive short-term permits but not the more expensive exclusive access permits. As McLain and Lynch (2010) stated, "Medium- and large-scale brush and shed operators acquire [the longer term] leases, and then sublet their harvesting rights to harvesters. The expectation was that harvesters would sell the products they took off the land to the shed holding the lease. In other cases, the shed operators sublet their harvesting rights to brush bosses, who organized crews of harvesters to do the work on the ground. Again, the leaseholder expected the brush boss and his crew members to sell their harvested materials to his shed." This arrangement has led to some concerns regarding employer-employee relationships (table 8).

Charging for permits has allowed landowners to earn income that covers some of the administrative costs of nontimber forest product harvesting on their lands (Lynch and McLain 2003). Such costs might include installing gates to regulate harvest, maintaining roads, and dealing with illegal dumping and vandalism.

Fines up to $1,000 can be issued by law enforcement if a harvester does not have a valid harvesting permit (McLain and Lynch 2010). Even so, many harvesters and buyers resist regulation because enforcement is expensive and difficult (Lynch and McLain 2003). Thomas and Schumann (1993) suggested that beargrass was among the most frequently poached items from national forests in the Pacific Northwest. In 1 year alone, more than 90 718 kg (100 tons) of beargrass leaves were illegally harvested on Oregons's Willamette National Forest (Mosley 2000 in Vance et al. 2004).

Economic Value of Commercial Beargrass Harvesting

The value of the floral greens industry in the Pacific Northwest (Oregon, Washington, and British Columbia) was estimated to be around $128 to $130 million in 1989 (Schlosser and Blatner 1997, Schlosser et al. 1991). By 2002, estimates had risen to $236 million (Daffan 2006). Estimates for beargrass alone differ widely. For example, Schlosser and Blatner estimated the 1997 value of beargrass to be over $1 million. By 2002, the combined value of beargrass and salal was estimated to be $54 million (Daffan 2006). Lack of long-term data from a consistent and reliable source makes it difficult to assess financial growth of the market over time, or to isolate the value of beargrass from the more generic floral greens industry.

The economic benefit to harvesters is equally difficult to estimate because the price offered for harvested beargrass differs significantly between seasons and buyers, depending on the quality of the beargrass, market demand, and product availability (Thomas and Schumann 1993). The highest prices are generally offered when beargrass availability is low (Hansis 1998). In 1991, bunches of beargrass sold from 20 cents to $1.60 per .45 kg (1 pound), depending on the month (Hansis 1998, Thomas and Schumann 1993). One buyer indicated that he might pay anywhere from $5,000 to $10,000 to a group of harvesters for material gathered over the course of a week (Thomas and Schumann 1993). In 1993, 4536 kg (10,000 pounds) of confiscated beargrass sold at auction for $4,750 (Thomas and Schumann 1993). Throughout the 1990s, individual harvesters reported making anywhere from $20 to $175 per day (Brown 2001, Hansis 1998, McLain and Lynch 2003).

Beargrass harvesting is by no means guaranteed to be a profitable enterprise. When producers offer low prices, it is a struggle for the harvester to offset the cost of a permit (Hansis 1998). If too many permits are sold, it is difficult for a harvester to gather enough material to offset the price of the permit (Lynch and McLain 2003). In addition, beargrass harvesters might have to purchase permits for transporting commercial quantities of beargrass on state highways and roads (Lynch and McLain 2003). Harvesters with access to transportation can charge harvesters without transportation fees from $5 to $10 to share transportation (Lynch and McLain 2003).

Additional Benefits and Costs of Commercial Beargrass Harvesting

Beargrass harvesting generally does not require an advanced skill set. Harvesters are not required to speak English, can avoid revealing the status of their citizenship, and are paid in cash (Brown 2001; Hansis 1996, 1998). These factors can make beargrass harvesting attractive for immigrant or undocumented workers (Brown 2001; Hansis 1996, 1998). Harvest work is generally available and harvesters may be able to bring their families (Brown 2001; Hansis 1996, 1998). However, many harvesters remarked to Brown (2001) that harvesting was physically hard and as a result it was uncommon for anybody to intensively harvest for more than 5 years (Brown 2001). Both Hansis (1996) and Brown (2001) have reported some instances of violence between nontimber forest harvesters or different forest user groups over access and ownership of resources.

Beargrass Disturbances

Disturbances are key drivers of ecosystem dynamics (Hutchinson 1953, Rixen et al. 2007). Knowledge about natural and human disturbance regimes contributes to adopting practices that maintain or restore ecosystem processes and functions, community structures, and cultural traditions (Brooks 2008, Peter and Shebitz 2006, Shebitz et al. 2008). The interactive effects of natural and human disturbances in beargrass habitat are not well understood. There is, however, literature on the effects of individual disturbances that we synthesize in this section.

Historical and contemporary land use practices in beargrass habitat, coupled with the rise of the commercial floral greens industry, are creating shifts in the disturbance regime of beargrass habitat. More specifically, beargrass is experiencing decreased disturbance from natural and anthropogenic fire (Peter and Shebitz 2006), and increased disturbance from leaf harvest by the floral industry (Thomas and Schumann 1993). The differences between these disturbance types and their potential effects on beargrass, its pollinators, and human gatherers are discussed below. Additional natural and anthropogenic disturbances that may also be contributing to patterns in beargrass distribution, abundance, reproduction, and leaf quality are also mentioned.

Fire

Fire as a natural disturbance—

Wildfire is an ecological process that influences plant community structure and function and is a major natural disturbance in western beargrass ecosystems (Agee 1993). Lightning is the primary source of ignition in forested landscapes of the Pacific Northwest, Rocky Mountains, and Sierra Nevada (Agee 1993, Barrett and Arno 1999, Keeley and Stephenson 2000), whereas volcanic activity, such as the eruption of Mount St. Helens, serves as a secondary ignition source (Barrett and Arno 1999). In general, storms are more frequent and influential causes of ignition in upland forest habitats than in coastal or valley areas (Boyd 1999).

In Oregon and the northern Rocky Mountains, natural fires occur more frequently in high-elevation forests and are less frequent in low-elevation forests and grasslands (Boyd 1999, Barrett and Arno 1999). Natural fires in the western mountains generally occur during the summer months (May to September), owing to their association with summer lightning storms (Bartuszvige and Kennedy 2009, Boyd 1999). Late-season fires (summer to fall) have also been reported in some areas, such as the eastern slopes of the Cascades (Wright and Agee 2004). In northern California, particularly inland portions of the region, the potential for lightning fires is highest during the period of especially hot, dry conditions occurring between August and October (Agee 1993).

Wildfire extent within the range of beargrass differs widely. In the Oregon Cascades, reports indicate areas burned from less than 10 ha (Morrison and Swanson 1990) to greater than 4000 ha (Wright and Agee 2004). In the Sierra Nevada, fire reports range in size from 1 to 800 ha (Bartuszvige and Kennedy 2009). Fire extent in high-elevation, subalpine habitat depends largely on the distribution and abundance of forest vegetation (fuel), because rock or snow fields may prevent the spread of fire across patchy forests (Agee 1993). At lower elevations, wet forests composed of less-flammable tree species can limit the spread of fire (Agee 1993). Fire extent is also strongly linked to weather patterns, with the tendency for large fires to coincide with periods of annual and seasonal drought (Wright and Agee 2004). Because natural fire regimes are closely tied to climate, elevation, forest community structure, and other environmental factors (Agee 1993), the frequency and severity of naturally occurring fire in beargrass habitat (by tree-ring records dating back 800 years) (Morrison and Swanson 1990) differ across the range of beargrass habitats, as detailed in table 9.

Fire as an anthropogenic disturbance—

Across the range of beargrass, Native Americans managed land with the aid of fire for centuries. The practice is more commonly documented at lower elevations and

Table 9—Natural fire patterns across ranges

Species composition	Range	Climate	Favorable fire conditions	Fire severity and frequency	Sources
Pacific silver fir (*Abies amabilis*), Douglas-fir (*Pseudotsuga menziesii*), and western hemlock (*Tsuga heterophylla*)	Western Cascades, low elevation	Temperate rain forest. Wet cool winter, dry summers	Drought conditions		Agee 1993, Morrison and Swanson 1990
Mountain hemlock (*Tsuga mertensiana*), subalpine fir (*Abies lasiocarpa*)	Western Cascades, high elevation	Montane/alpine	Drought conditions with east winds	Severe, stand-replacing, but infrequent. 300- to 600-year natural intervals	Agee 1993, Morrison and Swanson 1990
Ponderosa pine (*Pinus ponderosa*)	Eastern Cascades	Hot, dry summers and cool, wet winters. Prevailing winds and moisture come mainly from the West. The leeward, eastern slope lies in the rain shadow of the mountain range, and is significantly drier than the western side of the range	Fires triggered by high fuel build-ups owing to large insect outbreaks or longer than normal fire return intervals	Frequent fires every 1 to 43 years with occasional 25- to 100-year intervals. The less frequent, the more mixed the intensity	Agee 1993, Bartuszvige and Kennedy 2009
Mixed-conifer forests of grand fir (*Abies grandis*), white fir (*A. concolor*), and Douglas-fir	Eastern Cascades	Hot, dry summers and cool, wet winters. Prevailing winds and moisture come mainly from the West. The leeward, eastern slope lies in the rain shadow of the mountain range, and is significantly drier than the western side of the range	Fires triggered by high fuel build-ups owing to large insect outbreaks or longer than normal fire return intervals	Variable frequency and severity	Agee 1993, Bartuszvige and Kennedy 2009
Douglas-fir, western hemlock, and/or western redcedar (*Thuja plicata*)	Coastal region (west of Cascades)	The coastal forests of the Pacific Northwest are characterized by a moist, maritime climate	Moist, maritime climate limits the natural frequency and intensity of fires. Rare weather conditions (e.g., drought and high wind) foster the spread of fire in this environment	Natural fire regimes vary widely, fire intervals range from <50 years along the crest of the Coast Range in southern Oregon to as many as 750 years in moist, coastal forests of the northern Oregon Coast Range and the Olympic Mountains. Tend to be severe, stand-replacing crown fires	Agee 1993, Halpern and Spies 1995, Henderson et al. 1989, Peter and Shebitz 2006
Ponderosa pine, Douglas-fir, western larch (*Larix occidentalis*), and lodgepole pine	Rocky Mountains	Dry low-elevation to mesic higher elevations	Lightning ignition	Dry/low elevation = high frequency, low severity, with return intervals from 15 to 20 years Mesic/higher elevation = low-frequency, stand-replacing severity, 35- to 200-year return intervals	Barrett and Arno 1999, Bartuszvige and Kennedy 2009, Peet 2000
Mixed-conifer composition, including white fir, incense cedar (*Calocedrus* sp.), ponderosa pine, and Douglas-fir co-dominants	Sierra Nevada	Characterized by hot, dry summers and cool, wet winters, largely influenced by the Mediterranean climate of California	Lightning ignition	Mid elevation = high-frequency, low-intensity burns, interval of roughly 4 to 25 years	Barbour and Minnich 2000, Bartuszvige and Kennedy 2009, Keeley and Stephenson 2000

near areas inhabited prior to European settlement (Peter and Shebitz 2006, Shebitz et al. 2009). Unlike the relatively infrequent "natural" fires, indigenous burning in many areas was "regular, constant, and long term" (Boyd 1999, Peter and Shebitz 2006), altering natural fire regimes, decreasing fire return intervals, and causing cumulative effects in plant community structures and species distributions (Barrett and Arno 1999, Peter and Shebitz 2006, Wray and Anderson 2003). The Pacific Northwest has likely been inhabited by people for at least 10,000 years, and there is evidence that repeated anthropogenic burning for habitat management at some sites began at least 3,500 years ago (Peter and Shebitz 2006, Wray and Anderson 2003). In the Sierra Nevada, burning by humans began at least 9,000 years ago (Klinger et al. 2008), and in northern California, evidence points toward 8,000 years of anthropogenic burning, assuming that ancient inhabitants had a similar cultural lifestyle as more recent tribes (Rentz 2003).

Fire was one of the most important tools of Native Americans and was essential for a wide range of activities (Boyd 1999). Fire was used across landscapes to prevent outbreaks of potentially destructive natural fire, to facilitate travel and communication, for hunting, to promote and manage edible, medicinal, and textile plants and seed resources, including beargrass (see table 10 for a more detailed account of the varied purposes and functions of indigenous burning.)

Periodic burning of places where beargrass grows was used both to enhance its growth and to ensure its availability and quality for use in basketry (Hunter 1988; Rentz 2003; Shebitz et al. 2008, 2009a). Numerous western tribes including the Yurok, Karuk, Hupa, Chilula, Upland Takelma, and Olympic Peninsula tribes used periodic burning to maintain beargrass populations (Pullen 1996; Rentz 2003; Shebitz et al. 2008, 2009a). In the Pacific Northwest, the burning of beargrass sites also helped sustain habitat for bracken fern (*Pteridium aquilinum* (L.) Kuhn), camas (*Camassia quamash* (Pursh) Greene var. *azurea* (Heller) C.L. Hitchc.), and huckleberries (*Vaccinium* spp.), as well as other valuable plants, resulting in sites bountiful in many resources (Boyd 1999, Shebitz 2005). While indigenous burning was a common and widespread practice in the West, specific burn techniques, including timing, frequency, severity, and extent, differed depending on cultural needs and habitat characteristics of the region. During summer (July–August), fires allowed for beargrass rhizomes to form young new tillers in the fall immediately following the burn, and earlier and more growth by the following summer (table 10), which fostered longer, more useable leaf lengths (fig. 10).

Effects of fire on beargrass—
Beargrass is well adapted to recurrent burning, and can exhibit rapid and successful regrowth after fire (Boyd 1999, Maule 1959, Thomas and Schumann 1993). Indeed,

Table 10—Cultural burning for beargrass

Region	Timing	Frequency	Severity	Extent	Sources
Northern California/ Sierra Nevada	Late summer/early fall, following harvest of beargrass, after the first fall rains during rainy season.	Inhabited areas show a record of 5- to 20-year burn intervals.	Slow moving surface fires. Low to moderate intensity, controlled by removal of excess fuels prior to burning.	1-to 5-acre patches, rotating between adjacent areas of similar fuel and forest composition. See Six Rivers, Klamath, and Plumas National Forests in California.	Hunter 1988, Keeley and Stephenson 2000, Klinger et al. 2008 Rentz 2003
Olympic Peninsula —Skokomish	Conducted in the fall, after the first frost.	Annual rotating burn schedule, specific sites burned every 2 to 3 years. Open areas burned more frequently than peripheral areas.	Slow-moving surface fires.	Varies from a few square meters to hectares.	Peter and Shebitz 2006, Shebitz 2005, Shebitz et al. 2009a
Rocky Mountains	Fall/early spring, when ignition would not cause destructive forest fires. Few accounts of summer burning.	Tree ring analysis suggests that settled sites had uniform 9-year fire intervals, as opposed to the varying but approximate 18-year intervals at unsettled sites.	Low severity, crown fires not ignited by Native Americans.		Barrett and Arno 1999
Willamette Valley, Oregon	Late summer, early fall. No record of burning at any other time.		Early settlers described the region as "baptized in fire" and journeyed 20 miles across ash.		Boyd 1999

burning may benefit beargrass via reduced competition with shrubs and trees (Boyd 1999, Crane 1990) and via increased light and soil temperatures (Maule 1959). Fire is important for freeing mineral nutrients for plant uptake, and the increased availability of nutrients, like nitrogen, provides additional benefits to beargrass (Campbell et al. 2007, Ferrenberg et al. 2006, Rentz 2003).

Vegetative Reproduction, Percentage of Cover, and Leaf Characteristics

The primary fire adaptation of beargrass is its ability to sprout from underground rhizomes (Crane 1990). Shebitz et al. (2009a) found that beargrass leaves resprouted from rhizomes within 5 months of a high-severity fire, and Rentz (2003) reported that plants burned to the ground were once again covered with leaves the following summer. The short-term effects of prescribed burning (both low and high severity) and manual clearing on beargrass growth and reproduction (flowering, vegetative reproduction, and seedling establishment) were at least 2-year reductions in beargrass cover in the same study. High-severity burned sites had a significantly higher number of beargrass leaves than unburned control plots (Shebitz et al. 2009a). This finding is consistent with previous reports that beargrass initially decreases after a fire, especially hot broadcast burns (Crane 1990). The observed fire-induced increase in beargrass shoot density 2 years after burning (Shebitz et al. 2009a) is also consistent with previous observations and research. Maule (1959) reported that beargrass increased greatly in numbers as early as 2 years after a forest fire in the Washington Cascades, and grew densely in older burn sites. Likewise, in northern Idaho, after a light fire, beargrass increased to 11-percent cover after 10 years (Crane 1990). Following a Montana wildfire, beargrass resumed growth and reached 2-to 3-percent cover in 10 years (Crane 1990).

Fire history can affect the structural characteristics of beargrass leaves, as demonstrated by significant differences between leaves on plants previously exposed to fire versus leaves from unburned plants (Rentz 2003). Leaves collected from burned sites were narrower and thinner than those from unburned areas, and also more pliable, resulting from fewer hypodermal fiber rows below the adaxial surface and an overall reduction in sclerified tissue when compared to leaves from plants in unburned sites (Rentz 2003). The origin of structural leaf differences between unburned and burned plants has not been investigated, but the observed changes in leaf structure are likely either an internal physiological response to the removal of vegetative material or a response to postfire changes in environmental conditions, such as differences in soil moisture, nutrients (particularly nitrogen), or light availability at the leaf base (Rentz 2003).

Sexual Reproduction

Observational increases in beargrass flowering within 2 years following fire have been reported (Kruckeberg 2003, Maule 1959, Rentz 2003, Sullivan 2009). In contrast, Shebitz et al. (2009a) found no significant effect of high-severity burn on flowering over the 2-year monitoring period, and a decline in flowering after low-severity fire. This variability in results may be due to differences in site conditions and short-term allocation of photosynthate (Shebitz et al. 2009a).

Establishment and Survival

One greenhouse experiment found increased germination when seeds from low-elevation Washington sites were exposed to smoke-infused water (Shebitz et al. 2009b). In the field, broadcast beargrass seeds were found to germinate more readily after high-severity, duff-burning fires, and produced greater seedling establishment (Shebitz et al. 2009a). Because neither manually cleared nor low-severity burning affected beargrass seedling establishment, this study result is probably due to the exposure of mineral soil rather than to reduced competition. The mean germination rate of broadcast beargrass seed in high-severity burn plots was 9.2 percent after 1 year, compared to 0.7 percent in reference plots (Shebitz et al. 2009a). This result is consistent with Crane (1990) that in situations where hot surface fires kill beargrass rhizomes, beargrass seedlings can germinate and establish in areas with exposed soil. Surface fires do not consume the rhizomes of beargrass, but hot fires can damage its meristematic region, which is often positioned at or above the interface between organic material and mineral soil (Crane 1990, Shebitz 2010). This region is important for survival of the plant because it is the only portion of the rhizome able to produce new growth (Crane 1990). Under wet or moist conditions, the moisture held in the basal leaves will limit the transfer of heat to the meristem, but under dry conditions, leaves may increase the heat delivered to the base of the rosette. Additionally, if beargrass tussocks have accumulated leaf litter, they may continue to burn after a fire passes, further increasing the likelihood of meristematic damage and plant mortality (Shebitz et al. 2009a).

Low-severity fires have historically been used for beargrass habitat management (Hunter 1988, Peter and Shebitz 2006) because very high temperatures and long fire residence times associated with heavy fuel concentrations are most likely to cause beargrass mortality. In Rocky Mountain habitat types, beargrass is reported to increase after light broadcast fires, but to decrease after hot fires or scarification. In some habitat types, beargrass may not recover to prefire levels for more than 9 years after a severe fire (Crane 1990). In contrast, recent experiments by Shebitz et al. (2009a) found that high-severity fire resulted in the greatest increase in beargrass abundance after 1 and 2 years. Only high-severity fire was effective at preparing safe sites for beargrass seedling establishment, probably because beargrass seeds benefit from contact with mineral soil for germination and the litter layer remained intact after the low-severity burns. Likewise, only high-severity fire resulted in an increase in beargrass vegetative reproduction (shoot number), despite the fact that there was some beargrass mortality owing to rhizome meristem damage (Shebitz 2010). Beargrass populations may persist most successfully under mixed-severity fire regimes in the Pacific Northwest.

Effects of Fire Suppression on Beargrass

Not just fire, but also the suppression of fire can affect beargrass. Early Euro-American settlers had a strong antifire bias; it was viewed as undesirable and destructive. Concern grew over the hazards of fire for both inhabited areas and for the lumber industry (Rentz 2003). After several catastrophic western fires beginning in 1910, burning was prohibited within the national forests nationwide and the policy of fire suppression was established (Rentz 2003). **Also contributing to the decline in anthropogenic burning of beargrass habitat was the** forced relocation of Native Americans to reservations (Boyd 1999, Peter and Shebitz 2006, Shebitz 2005). The mentality that fire was a destructive force to be contained or eliminated persisted into the 1960s, when the beneficial effects of fire on plants, animals, and ecological interactions began to be recognized by scientists and the field of fire ecology developed (Barrett and Arno 1999).

The decline of anthropogenic burning and the suppression of natural fire have led to the decline of many beargrass prairies and savannas in the Rocky Mountains and Pacific Northwest (Shebitz et al. 2008, Wray and Anderson 2003). On the Olympic Peninsula, traditional burning practices stopped around 1877. Meanwhile, the moist maritime climate of the peninsula does not support the frequency of natural fire required to maintain beargrass savannas (Peter and Shebitz 2006). The restriction of anthropogenic fire across beargrass habitat has, therefore, resulted in forest succession over former beargrass prairies and savannas (Peter and Shebitz 2006, Shebitz 2005, Shebitz et al. 2008) with corresponding changes in plant communities that can reduce availability of usable basket materials (Rentz 2003). Although prescribed burns that mimic presettlement conditions are now increasingly included in forestry management plans in the Northwest (Anderson 2005, Boyd 1999, Hunter 1988), and indigenous and culturally prescribed burning for beargrass is done in some areas (Anderson 2005, Rentz 2003, Senos et al. 2006), fire suppression and prevention policies continue to restrict the ability of Native Americans to burn vegetation in conjunction with harvesting beargrass and other cultural resources.

Beargrass is one resource typically collected from burned areas that is declining over at least some of its range (Hunter 1988, Shebitz 2005, Shebitz et al. 2008). Change in plant community composition is a readily documented ecological consequence of fire-suppression practices. Anthropogenic systems, such as indigenous, fire-maintained beargrass habitat, tend to follow certain successional trajectories once active fire management has ceased (Peter and Shebitz 2006). In the Pacific Northwest maritime region, many previously open beargrass meadows are now covered with Douglas-fir (Boyd 1999, Peter and Shebitz 2006, Shebitz et al. 2009a), or western hemlock/salal/beargrass (*Tsuga mertensiana* (Bong.) Carrière/ *Gaultheria* sp./*X. tenax*) or similar plant associations (Henderson et al. 1989 in Peter and Shebitz 2006). At higher elevations, former beargrass savanna sites are now dominated by a mix of lodgepole pine and Douglas-fir (Peter and Shebitz 2006).

Effects of Fire Disturbance on Pollinator Community

Fire shapes many environments, including beargrass ecosystems (Peter and Shebitz 2006). The potential effects of fire management on arthropod communities are variable and can have both beneficial and detrimental effects (Swengel 2001).

The creation of suitable habitat via the large sunlit openings in the forest canopy is perhaps the most important benefit of fire to insect pollinators (Hartley et al. 2007). Pollinating insects generally rely on sunlight to raise their body temperature enough to make flight permissible, thus increased sunlight in burned habitat may attract these insects (Campbell et al. 2007). Fire-created canopy openings also provide environments where herbaceous vegetation (pollinator food plants) can flourish owing to increased light levels and reduced competition from trees and shrubs (Huntzinger 2003, Kerstyn and Stiling 1999).

As a result of fire-induced changes in vegetation architecture, changes in nectar and pollen energy rewards also occur following fire, reflecting a general shift from annuals (mostly low-reward open access flowers) to perennials (mostly high-reward restricted access flowers) as post-fire regeneration ensues (Potts et al. 2003). Pollen production (measured as the number of pollen grains per unit area) has been found to be highest in freshly burnt sites and decreases with time (measured up to 50 years) (Potts et al. 2003). Although such measurements have not been made on beargrass or its ecosystems, the highly variable effects of fire on beargrass flowering patterns suggest that beargrass pollen energy, per area, would likely decrease or remain unchanged during the first few years after burning, following which it would be expected to increase relative to unburned sites (Maule 1959, Shebitz et al. 2009a) (fig. 10).

Many studies have found a negative or mixed response of invertebrates to fire (Black et al. 2007, Harper et al. 2000, Swengel 2001). Fire has the potential to negatively influence pollinators and other arthropods in two major ways: directly, by fire-related mortality, and indirectly, by reducing, eliminating, or otherwise altering floral resources, vegetation, arthropod prey, litter, duff, woody debris, and other habitat elements pertaining to shelter or food (Campbell et al. 2007, Ferrenberg et al. 2006). Not surprisingly, there is loss of pollinators and other insects immediately following a substantial burn (Potts et al. 2003, Swengal 2001). Such reductions, for some taxonomic groups, may last only for a short period however (Potts et al. 2003).

According to Vance et al. (2004), syrphid flies and flower-visiting beetles are the most abundant pollinators of beargrass, while members of various bee families appear to play a less prominent role. Although a substantial number of studies have examined the effects of fire on arthropods (e.g., Harper et al. 2000, Hartley et al. 2007, Johnson et al. 2008), the majority of these studies used collection methods

Steve Levy

Figure 10—Beargrass leaves form a clump at the base of the inflorescence and are readily visible in late-season and postfire landscapes.

(e.g., pitfall traps, sweep-netting of vegetation) that are not suitable for capturing pollinator species (more readily collected in colored pan traps, colored malaise traps, or directly from flowers) (Campbell et al. 2007, Vance et al. 2004). Hence, although the effect of fire on floral communities and associated rewards has clear implications for pollinator community structure (Potts et al. 2003), the effects of fire on pollinators, specifically, are relatively understudied (Campbell et al. 2007) (fig. 11). In general, fire studies pertaining to beargrass pollinator guilds highlight the benefit of periodic fire on the diversity and abundance of these groups (table 11).

Steve Levy

Figure 11—The effects of disturbances in beargrass ecosystems on pollinators such as beetles are not well understood.

Table 11—Response of beargrass pollinators to fire

Classification	Response to fire	Sources
Order: Diptera Major family: Syrphidae (hover flies)	Syrphid flies exhibit significantly greater abundance in plots that have been treated with high heat fire. Syrphid abundance has been negatively correlated with change in tree density (measured as basal area) and positively correlated with percentage of herbaceous plant cover, with the latter explaining 70 percent of the variation in the abundance data. Syrphids may benefit from fire-induced increases in herbaceous plant cover, probably owing to increases in available food sources for both adults (pollen and nectar) and larvae (e.g., aphids, dead wood).	Campbell et al. 2007, Reemer 2005
Order: Coleoptera Major family: Cerambycidae (long-horn beetles)	Fire creates logs and many standing dead and dying trees which serve as hospitable feeding habitat for insect pollinators with tree-boring larval stages, such as cerambycids. Many beetle species are highly adapted to fire conditions (through sense organs sensitive to infrared wavelengths of fire and through wax glands protecting against desiccation). Scorched ponderosa pine trees are particularly susceptible to beetles and often suffer post-fire insect attack. Beetle pollinators as a whole have exhibited significantly greater abundance and richness in plots that have been treated with hot fire. Increases in dead wood, herbaceous plant abundance and richness, or exposure of the mineral soil may have contributed to the greater beetle numbers in burned areas.	Agee 1993, Campbell et al. 2007, Ferrenberg et al. 2006, Swengel 2001, Werner 2002
Order: Coleoptera Major family: Meloidae (blister beetles)	Fire may have indirect impacts on beetle pollinators with predatory stages, such as meloid beetles, by increasing or decreasing the abundance of specific prey.	Capinera 2008, Kerstyn and Stiling 1999
Order: Apoidea (bees) Major families: Andrenidae Apidae Halictidae Megachilidae	Owing to the high mobility of adults and their rapid ability to recolonize burned habitats, fire may have relatively less negative impact on bee populations. In temperate hardwood forests and pine forests with Mediterranean climates, abundance and species diversity of some bees was highest at recently (within 1 to 3 years) burned sites and declined with elapsed time post fire. Freshly burnt areas supported 20 to 25 bee species per site, while intermediate and mature areas supported only 7 to 12 species. (Patterns in abundance and species richness closely mirror the abundance and richness of the flowering plant community.) Bees have been found to be most abundant after high-temperature fires (which also result in species-rich understory vegetation). Hotter fires may also provide more bare-ground habitat for ground-nesting bees. Freshly burned sites are characterized by bee species that start and finish flying late in the season and bear multiple generations per year, and by short-tongued, solitary, low-dispersal species.	Black et al. 2007, Campbell et al. 2007, Michener 1979, Moretti et al. 2009, Potts et al. 2003

Harvest by Native Americans

Traditional use of beargrass by Native Americans in basketry seems to have mostly benefited the plant because historical management practices (anthropogenic burning) were intended to encourage the plant's establishment (see "Seasonality and Location of Native American Harvest"). Leaves for use in basketry are typically harvested 1 to 3 years following a burn (Hunter 1988, Shebitz et al. 2009a, Vance et al. 2001), as their quality for use in basketry improves after burning (Rentz 2003). Specific harvest season seems to differ across the range: on the Olympic Peninsula in the late fall and winter (Vance et al. 2001), and in California during late June to August, depending on site factors that affect soil moisture and leaf growth. Harvest time is likely subject to the seasonality of fire. In northwestern California, harvesting is done by pinching and pulling a tight core of packed leaves (tuffs) and then slapping them on a sturdy surface (e.g., thigh or other hand) to separate the compacted leaf bases (yellowish-white tissue). From this clump of now mostly separated individual leaves, the center-most threadlike ones are removed, as well as any unsuitable "Frog woman" thicker and wider red-edged ones (see box on page 47). The mid-size and larger supple leaves are then sorted and laid to dry on mats or tarps in the sun (fig. 9). Some weavers sort leaves by similar sizes after drying. For example, by leaf width (size classes) as an overlay to match the width/diameter of the conifer (ponderosa pine or sitka spruce (*Picea sitchensis* Bong.) root used in twine weaving style. Leaves not suitable for use in basketry (brittle blades or blades with yellow tips or paling color) are typically avoided (LaLande and Pullen 1999, Rentz 2003, Shebitz 2005, Shebitz et al. 2009a, Vance et al. 2001) and there is a general taboo against harvesting more material than can be used (Bennett and Shaw 1987), which reduces the likelihood of overharvest.

Environmental effect of harvest disturbance—
As discussed previously, Native Americans periodically burned beargrass habitat to enhance the growth of beargrass and improve its viability for use in basketry, and to ensure long-term availability. Over time, this burning has resulted in the establishment and persistence of vegetative communities in locations where they might not otherwise exist (Boyd 1999 in Shebitz et al. 2009a). Owing to the long history of anthropogenic burning, it is likely that beargrass now belongs to a fire-dependent ecosystem, inherently unstable now that management practices have changed (Peter and Shebitz 2006).

Effects of disturbances on traditional harvesters—
Any disturbance that results in a decline of beargrass will have a corresponding negative effect on traditional harvesters who gather blades for use in basketry. On the Olympic Peninsula, traditional harvesters have reported a decline in the availability of beargrass suitable for basketry (Peter and Shebitz 2006, Shebitz 2005, Shebitz et al. 2008). Contemporary weavers from northern California also express difficulty obtaining beargrass, noticing both a decline in quantity and quality (Anderson 2005). This decline in suitable material is primarily attributed to the plants no longer being burned (Anderson 2005); however, a variety of other factors are also mentioned by contemporary weavers including increased harvest by commercial harvesters and disruption to beargrass habitat from commercial logging.

Karuk story (adapted by Frank K. Lake)

Frog (Western Toad) woman went with the women and girls along the river and creeks to collect materials when she was learning to weave baskets. But frog did not want to go with them to harvest beargrass up in the mountains during the hot summer days. Instead, she stayed by the river and used mostly sand bar willow shoots and roots in her weaving. When it came time for frog to overlay design materials on the willow base, she had black (maiden hair fern stems) and red (woodwardia-chainfern dyed with alder bark), but no white (beargrass lily leaves). By now it was fall, with the days growing shorter and cooler. Frog woman finally went up the trail following the ridge to the upper Douglas-fir and pine forests. It was too late, however. Frog woman did not know how to collect fresh younger tillers—or "tuffs"—of formerly burned plants. When she finally found beargrass clumps and pulled on leaves to harvest then, she cut her hand and her blood ran down in to the center of the clump. Now to this day, you better learn how to collect at the right time of the year and the correct plant parts (younger leaf bundles-tillers) that were properly burned the year before. People who don't know better use "Frog woman's" type of leaves in their baskets and they are inferior and tough as well as sharp and reddish along the edges.

Concerns over the harvest of beargrass for the floral greens industry are often linked to the industry's dependence on seasonal immigrant labor. Seasonal harvesters operate with little to no training and may damage the plant through indiscriminant harvest practices (Hansis 1998, Shebitz 2005, Shebitz et al. 2008). There is also a growing concern over the volume of the commercial harvest (Schlick 1994) and the possibility that future harvest pressure created by the floral greens industry will lead to illegal harvesting on public and tribal lands, especially as demand grows and access to public lands becomes more difficult (Brown 2000). Some tribal members reported an increased level of illegal harvesting (Brown and Marin-Hernández 2000, Shebitz 2005, Shebitz et al. 2008). For example, on the Olympic National Forest, tribe members reported seeing truckloads of beargrass despite the fact that the forest was not issuing harvesting permits to nontribal members (Shebitz 2008). U.S Code Title 25 (2011) declared "there is a serious threat to Indian forest lands arising from trespass and unauthorized harvesting of Indian forest land resources (National Indian Forest Resources Management Act 2006).

Native American harvesters also worry that logging is affecting what once served as beargrass habitat (Shebitz et al. 2008). Lynch and McLain (2003) and Schilich (1994) found that some tribe members expressed concern that the use of pesticides and aerial sprays in forestry practices could diminish the quality of beargrass otherwise suitable for basketry.

The Floral Greens Industry

Harvest method—

Commercial harvesters in theory remove only a handful of the longest blades from the center of the plant (Crane 1990, Lynch and McLain 2003, Schlosser et al. 1992, Thomas and Schumann 1993). Harvest occurs by hand-pulling the leaf blade from its sheath, or by using a knife to cut the leaves. Harvesters attempt to remove as much of the leaf blade as possible to meet the length requirement set by purchasing sheds. The harvested leaves are bound together in .22 kg to .45 kg (half-pound to one pound) bunches, bagged in quantities of about 45.3 kg (100 pounds), and removed from the woods for cleaning and sorting (Thomas and Schumann 1993).

Commercial harvesters typically concentrate in a particular area, harvest all available beargrass, then return home to clean and sell the harvested material (Thomas and Schumann 1993). Harvest occurs primarily in wilderness or other public land owing to the difficulty of cultivating beargrass.

Environmental effect of harvest—

Beargrass commercial harvest is currently monitored through a permit system. This means it monitors the number of harvesters rather than the volume of material harvested (see "Permitting and Regulation"). Such a system can allow individuals to overharvest a particular area. Geographically stable, long-term harvesters tend to be concerned about regeneration, but more numerous short-term or migrant harvesters are not (Brown 2001, Hansis 1998). Furthermore, the confusion and expense that surround the beargrass harvest permit system has led to illegal harvesting in many areas (Lynch and McLain 2003). Poor harvesting practices can lead to extensive damage if the core of the plant is cut and flowering shoots are destroyed (Vance et al. 2004). The plant regenerates slowly once the core has been cut (Kramer 2001, Thomas and Schuman 1993).

Effects of disturbances on commercial harvesters—

Much of the disturbance that commercial harvesters face is created internally. Long-term, geographically stationary harvesters tend to worry about-long term effects of overharvesting, the growing numbers of illegal harvesters, and the effect of poor harvesting techniques often practiced by untrained harvesters (Brown

2001). Self-proclaimed "good pickers" worry that they will be penalized along with damaging pickers by increased monitoring and higher permit prices (Lynch and McLain 2003). Unpermitted harvesters create tension with permitted harvesters (Brown 2001, Lynch and McLain 2003), and the practice of issuing unlimited permits for a single area heightens competition and promotes adversarial relationships among commercial harvesters who fear they will be unable to harvest enough material to pay for the permit (Lynch and McLain 2003). There has also been growing animosity between cultural groups as well as groups of commercial harvesters over access to particularly favorable plots (Hansis 1996, Lynch and McLain 2003). Tension between commercial harvesters, as well as between harvesters and other forest user groups such as hunters, has prompted some harvesters to begin carrying weapons (Hansis 1996, 1998). Beargrass pickers often feel that they are blamed for the negative behaviors of other user groups, and punished by restricted access, which fuels this tension (Kramer 2001, Lynch and McLain 2003).

An emerging, less-documented worry related to commercial access is that the labor market is trending toward the issuing of exclusive access permits (Hansis 1998, Lynch and McLain 2003, Thomas and Schuman 1993). While this might resolve access disputes, it is also likely that permits will become more expensive, and access for the small scale harvester could be restricted as a result (Lynch and McLain 2003).

Effects of harvest disturbance on pollinator community—Similar to herbivory (e.g., by grazing animals and insects), leaf harvest by humans directly decreases the amount of photosynthetic tissue of a plant has, thereby reducing the plant's available and potential resources for growth, reproduction, and survival (Cardel and Koptur 2010). Potential plastic responses of plants to herbivory (and presumably leaf harvest) include changes in resource allocation by the plant and changes in the quality and number of pollen grains produced owing to nutrient stress (Cardel and Koptur 2010). Harvest-driven plant mortality or suppression of flowering could result in patchier resources for pollinators, which, depending on the availability and proximity of other acceptable resources, may need to expend more foraging energy or reduce their intake of pollen food. Increased energy demands and decreased food supply both could negatively affect the reproductive success of pollinators. Considering that the availability of beargrass pollen to insects is already limited by the light and temperature requirements for the production of flowering stalks (Maule 1959), and by grazing ungulates who consume whole flowering stalks (Vance et al. 2004), harvest-driven losses in pollen resources may be significant. The overall effect of beargrass harvest on pollinators is unknown.

Additionally, beargrass harvest activity has the potential to degrade pollinator habitat, alter the vegetation community, and even kill individual pollinators as a result of trampling by humans or vehicle use on open sites (Black et al. 2011). Although beargrass itself is tolerant of trampling owing to its tough, wiry leaves and tufted growth habit (Crane 1990), some pollinators, particularly ground-nesting species, may not be so tolerant. Of course, owing to the mutual relationship between pollinators and beargrass, any negative effects on pollinators may, in turn, affect beargrass via a reduction in pollen grain deposition on stigmas in an already compatible-pollen limited system (Vance et al. 2004).

Timber Harvest

Timber harvest is a widespread anthropogenic disturbance in the Pacific Northwest and Rocky Mountains, and has resulted in extensive loss, fragmentation, and alteration of forested ecosystems throughout the range of beargrass (Halpern and Spies 1995). Although forest management practices in these regions differ depending on land ownership, site conditions, vegetation characteristics, and the period during which stands were harvested, logging has been extensive in many low- to-mid-elevation sites (Halpern and Spies 1995). Old-growth forests in Washington, Oregon, and California have declined in area by more than 50 percent since the 1950s (Halpern and Spies 1995).

Logging activites in beargrass habitat can alter succession and influence the diversity, abundance, and composition of understory vegetation over both the short and long term (Battles et al. 2001, Halpern and Spies 1995). Although canopy openings, increased light levels, and higher soil temperatures resulting from logging could potentially benefit beargrass growth and reproduction (Brockway et al. 1983, Maule 1959, Vance et al. 2001) most studies have found that logging-related activities result in both short- and long-term reductions in beargrass densities (Shebitz et al. 2009a). In a short-term Oregon Cascade Range study examining plant cover and composition (1) prior to clearcut logging, (2) after logging but before broadcast slash burning, and (3) during each of five growing seasons following burning, beargrass disappeared immediately after clearcut logging, remained absent after burning, and reappeared only in trace amounts 4 years later (Dyrness 1965). Clearcutting followed by broadcast burning strongly decreased the abundance of beargrass in a study conducted in high-elevation old-growth Douglas-fir forests of the Oregon and Washington Cascade Ranges. The study found that beargrass did not recover its prior abundance for more than 20 years (Halpern and Spies 1995). Similarly, beargrass recovery was found to take up to 23 years after clearcutting and broadcast burning in the grand fir/Oregon boxleaf association in northern Idaho (Crane

1990). Arno et al. (1985) reported that beargrass abundance decreased sharply after scarification following logging, and could take at least 25 years to recover or not recover at all (Arno et al. 1985).

Soil compaction, damage to rhizomes, and competition with understory plants have all been attributed to beargrass decline following logging-related disturbance (Arno et al. 1985, Crane 1990, Laursen 1984, Shebitz et al. 2008). Dryness (1965) reported that invasive species increased in frequency and percentage of cover after logging and burning, while many residual, previously widely-distributed plant species such as beargrass declined or disappeared altogether.

Logging-related changes in soil composition may also affect beargrass in sites harvested for timber. Unlike fire, tree harvest is a disturbance that removes rather than consumes vegetation, particularly if the slash is not left onsite. As a result, nutrients stored in the vegetation are not recycled in the system, and the influx of nutrients available to understory plants such as beargrass may be lower and different in composition than in burned or undisturbed forests (Bartuszvige and Kennedy 2009).

Logging could further affect beargrass by increasing erosion and landslide potential at beargrass sites. In Oregon, disturbances from the creation of logging roads and timber harvest activities have been documented that increase the frequency of landslides and erosion to a degree that is several times greater in clearcut areas than in forested areas (Swanson and Dyrness 1975).

Impacts of logging on commercial and traditional beargrass harvest—
Canopy density is correlated with the length, color, and thickness of beargrass leaves; canopy densities of less than 60 percent have been reported not to produce beargrass of commercially harvestable quality (Higgins et al. 2004). As a result, beargrass commercial harvest may be limited by overstory forest conditions and forest management practices (Schlosser and Blatner 1997). According to Laursen (1984), shelterwood or selection cuts are better than clearcuts for promoting beargrass growth. Beargrass is not typically commercially harvested from stands after a clearcut or a seed tree harvest until a closed forest canopy reoccurs and persists (Schlosser and Blatner 1997). If a shelterwood regeneration system occurs with the entries, observations suggest that beargrass harvest can occur after the first harvest entry, but not the others.

Timber harvest is also influencing traditional harvest potential in some areas. For example, in the Olympic Peninsula of Washington, a decline in beargrass owing to timber clearcuts is limiting the ability of Native Americans to access and harvest beargrass (Shebitz 2005). Charlotte Kalama, a Quinault elder and renowned basketmaker who has experienced difficulty getting basket-quality beargrass for a number of years, stated: "My husband used to get it for me, but it's hard to find now. Where he used to go, they have cut the trees. Now, beargrass grows short there, it stays [too] small" (Shebitz 2005).

Impact of logging on beargrass pollinators—
Similar to fire, certain logging-related disturbances may increase the abundance of insect pollinators by increasing the availability of distressed, dying, or dead trees. A study by O'Neill et al. (2008) in Montana lodgepole pine forests investigated the effects of shelterwood logging on wood-boring beetle pollinators and found that logged sites had increased abundance of adult cerambycids (including *Cosmosalia chrysocoma*, the most abundant of beargrass beetle pollinators) relative to unlogged plots and meadows. One year after logging, the abundance of cerambycids was similar among treatments (meadows, unlogged, and shelterwood logged plots), but 2 years after logging, cerambycid counts were highest in the shelterwood areas, and remained so throughout the 4-year duration of the study (although after 3 years the abundance values of the different treatements started to converge). The logging-related increases in cerambycid abundance may be attributed to the greater abundance of decaying wood (larval food) and flowers (adult food) in the recently logged areas (O'Neill et al. 2008). Likewise, saproxylic syrphid flies may also increase postlogging (Reemer 2005), as a result of both larval dependence on dead/dying trees and adult dependence on floral food resources.

Invasive Species

Nonnative invasive species are responsible for a wide array of economic and ecological damage to natural and managed ecosystems. About 42 percent of the plant and animal species on the threatened or endangered species lists in the United States are at risk primarily because of invasive species (Morse et al. 1995, Pimentel et al. 2005). Nonnative invasive plants are characteristically adaptable and aggressive, and have a high reproductive capacity, threatening native species by competing for light, nutrients, space, water, and pollinators, and by altering soil chemistry, natural fire regimes, and community structure (Pimentel et al. 2005).

The exposure of beargrass populations to invasive species is largely influenced by site elevation, canopy cover, and disturbance. High-elevation sites are relatively protected from invasive species owing to (1) minimal human activity and limited potential for propagule spread by humans, and (2) harsh climates and environmental conditions correlated with elevation, such as reduced moisture, low temperatures, and short growing seasons (Klinger et al. 2006, 2008; Randall et al. 1998). According to a recent evaluation by Anzinger and Radosevich (2008), coastal

Douglas-fir forests in the Pacific Northwest are more threatened by invasive species (particularly Scotch broom (*Cytisis scoparius* (L.) Link)) than are montane forests and meadows in this region. Hairy catsear (*Hypochaeris radicata* L.) is the only species listed as having realized or potential threat at higher elevation sites, and is considered of low threat (Anzinger and Radosevich 2008).

Root Diseases

Fungal root diseases in forested habitat result in patches of dead and dying trees, which, upon falling or dying back, create openings in the forest canopy (Hagle et al. 2003). Root diseases may therefore be important to beargrass because they create conditions with increased light levels and soil temperatures relative to closed canopy conditions.

Laminated root rot (*Phellinus weirii*), Armillaria root disease (*Armillaria ostoyae*), and Annosus root disease (*Heterobasidion annosum*) are three of the most common fungal root pathogens in the Pacific Northwest and Rocky Mountains (Dekker-Robertson et al., n.d.; Hagle et al. 2003). Trees of all sizes and ages may be killed by these diseases, although pathogen-specific susceptibility varies greatly among tree species (Hagle et al. 2003). With regard to forested beargrass habitat, grand fir forests are affected by all three of these diseases; Douglas-fir habitats are most likely to be affected by laminated root rot and Armillaria root disease; western hemlock forests are highly susceptible to Annosus root disease and moderately susceptible to laminated root rot; subalpine fir habitats are highly susceptible to Armillaria and moderately susceptible to both laminated root rot and Annosus; white and red fir forests are highly susceptible to Armillaria; mountain hemlock forests are highly susceptible to Annosus; and both lodgepole pine and western white pine habitats are moderately susceptible to Annosus (Dekker-Robertson et al., n.d.; Hagle et al. 2003).

Root diseases may also have significant impacts on beargrass pollinators. Similar to fire and logging, fungal diseases increase the availability of distressed, dying, and dead trees, thus creating habitat for wood-loving pollinator guilds such as wood-boring beetles, saproxylic hover flies, and wood-nesting bees. The canopy openings caused by root disease may further attract pollinators by providing warmer foraging conditions, and by promoting the flowering of beargrass and other species.

Avalanches and Landslides

Avalanche disturbance is an important driver in many subalpine forest ecosystems (Rixon et al. 2007). Snow avalanches are common and widespread geomorphic processes in the western mountains (Gao and Butler 1992) and may thus be a significant natural disturbance at high-elevation beargrass sites, although no known research is available as to the extent of this disturbance or its effects on beargrass.

Depending on frequency and severity, avalanches probably differ in their effects on this plant. Severe avalanches (i.e., those entraining ice, rocks, trees, and other material downslope) would damage or destroy any beargrass populations in their path, at least over the short term, while avalanches of less severity (i.e., small masses of flowing snow) may have less negative, or even beneficial, effects. Because beargrass is a relatively disturbance-tolerant plant capable of growth and survival in both forested and open habitats (Crane 1990, Maule 1959) and can regenerate from rhizomes following disturbance (Adams et al. 1987, Shebitz 2009a), it may suffer less from avalanches than other members of its community.

Landslides are also a common occurrence in both undisturbed and logged areas of the western mountains, and may be a significant disturbance in some beargrass habitat (Swanson and Dyrness 1975). In a study investigating plant community recovery following the 1980 volcanic eruption of Mount St. Helens, beargrass was among over 20 species found to regenerate from fragments and plant parts transported on root wads, stumps, and soil down a mud flow or debris slide. Beargrass regeneration, in this case, was by rhizomes, and no seedling establishment was recorded (Adams et al. 1987). Overall, beargrass appears to have evolved adequate responses to survive avalanches and landslides (Adams et al. 1987), although the effects of these disturbances on beargrass growth and reproduction are unknown.

Management and Research Considerations for Beargrass Ecosystems

Beargrass has multiple ecological and sociocultural roles (table 12). Although it is not listed as federally threatened or endangered and is still found across much of the range mapped for it in the 1950s, the plant is declining in some areas. Some associated ecosystem services and values are being affected as natural and anthropogenic disturbance regimes change. The main services at risk are traditional Native American uses and their associated cultural roles. Furthermore, there are probable effects to commercial harvesters in some locations and ecosystem processes associated with pollination may also be of concern.

Land management practices to conserve ecosystem diversity, services, and values require knowledge about how natural and anthropogenic disturbances interact to affect them in places where they are a concern. These interactions will differ across the range of a species; it follows that the best conservation management practices will also differ. What does this mean for management practices to conserve beargrass ecosystems? One implication is that management needs and approaches will differ according to local conditions and tribal customs because the services and values at risk in one location may be less of a concern elsewhere. For example, documented concerns about insufficient beargrass leaves for Indian basketry are associated with the Pacific Northwest, but not with the Rocky Mountain portion of its range.

This section summarizes the main social, cultural, environmental, ecological, and economic issues relating to the management of beargrass and the forested ecosystems in which it grows. It identifies circumstances in which management practices may differ or be in conflict for different resource objectives as well as topics for research that could aid management decisions.

Social and Cultural Considerations

Social and cultural considerations include the following:

- Beargrass grows together with other culturally, economically, or biologically important plant species on lands managed by different owners who may have different management objectives.
- Beargrass has traditionally been used by Native Americans for basketry material and ceremonial regalia and is an important element of maintaining their culture and identity.
- Management practices that incorporate local or traditional ecological knowledge and tribal management practices (e.g, anthropogenic burning) may help conserve biocultural diversity associated with beargrass ecosystems.
- Commercial harvesters differ in several social and cultural ways from one another and from traditional harvesters, including site transience vs. permanence. Enforcement and commercial permit compliance pertaining to laborer safety and rights are insufficient.

Environmental Considerations

Environmental considerations include the following:

- The overstory light environment in which beargrass grows affects how the plant reproduces and the number and properties of its leaves. It is unclear how different drivers of the plant light environment (fire, tree death via pathogens, insects, harvest or other disturbances) affect its reproduction and leaf properties. Deep and persistent shade alters leaf properties and plant morphology and likely results in decreased plant fitness.

Table 12—Beargrass management considerations[a]

Ecosystem role	Value at risk?	Associated plant part/ properties	Conditions that favor desirable plant properties	Disturbances that negatively affect value
Social:				
Native American basketry	Yes	Leaves: long, thin, pliable, strong, less pigment	• Partial canopy/ partial shade • Higher elevations • Recently burned areas	Anthropogenic: • Suppression of Indian burning and naturally-occurring fire • Commercial beargrass harvesting Natural: • Succession to late-seral forest
Commercial floral greens industry	In some parts of range	Leaves: deep green, long, wide, firm, >71 cm in length	• 60 to 90 percent canopy cover • Higher elevation conifer forest in later stages of succession	Anthropogenic: • Overharvesting beargrass • Silvicultural practices that create large canopy openings, reducing shade • Prescribed fire Natural: • Wildland fire
Aesthetic/spiritual Native American ceremonial regalia	Yes	Flowers (Leaves: similar requirements as basketry, above)	• Best flowering occurs in open conditions	Anthropogenic: • Trampling, commercial harvesting Natural: • Processes that favor vegetative state and suppress flowering state
Ecological:				
Food	No	Flowers, leaf base and leaves, pollen	• Partial canopy, open or diffuse light	Anthropogenic: • Suppression of Indian burning and naturally-occurring fire • Overharvesting beargrass Natural: • Processes that favor vegetative state and suppress flowering state (e.g., closed forest canopy)
Habitat and soil structure	No	Basal leaves, leaves, and rhizomes	• Diffuse light or shade	Anthropogenic: • Timber harvest practices that result in soil compaction and plant death
Pollination, decomposition	Yes	Aggregated flowers with nutrient-rich pollen	• Partial canopy, open or diffuse light, dead or dying trees that provide substrate for invertebrate pollinators and decomposers like longhorn beetles	Anthropogenic: • Suppression of fire Natural: • Succession to late-seral forest

[a] It should be noted that although indigenous use of fire in maintaining habitats is inarguable, the details of traditional burning strategies are often not clear (Wray and Anderson 2003). In some tribal groups, understanding of burning techniques and ecosystem effects was specialized knowledge, possessed by only a few individuals, and thus may not have been passed down through time.

- The current distribution of beargrass is not well documented, and it is unknown how its range is changing.

Ecosystem Considerations

Ecosystem considerations include:

- The identity and status of pollinator species in beargrass habitat has been identified in some areas, but across the plant's range the status of pollinators is unknown.
- The fitness of beargrass populations depends on periodic intervals in which the plant flowers and cross-pollination can occur. This implies phases in which overstory light conditions are suitable for flowering and there are sufficient masses of beargrass plants with adequate pollen to attract pollinators.
- Some beetle pollinators of beargrass are decomposers of dead and decaying wood.
- Beargrass provides food for animals large and small.
- The contribution of above- and belowground plant structure to soil and habitat properties is not well understood.

Economic Considerations

Economic considerations include:

- The changing dynamics, structure, and drivers of the floral greens industry are poorly understood or documented. A coordinated effort is lacking among landowners to monitor the amount of harvested beargrass being removed from specific locations.

- There is a lack of long-term price data for beargrass sold into the floral greens industry.

- Harvest of beargrass is tracked by permits issued rather than by volume collected. The workforce of harvesters in the floral greens industry is influenced by changing labor conditions in other sectors, and by changes in immigration policy.

- Price trends in the commercial beargrass industry appear to be consumer-driven rather than influenced by producers. As export of beargrass from the Pacific Northwest increases in importance, price trends are also influenced by international trade barriers and European market regulations and preferences.

Beargrass Management Considerations

Beargrass management considerations include:

- Different leaf properties (color, length, and pliability) are desired by different harvesters (see table 12). Dense forest overstory conditions appear to limit the abundance of beargrass plants and inhibit beargrass flowering, and thus management activities that promote canopy openings are expected to favor this species and its associated pollinators.

- Beargrass grows with other culturally important plants; management activities that favor one species may be beneficial, neutral, or harmful to others. The intentional use of fire to manage beargrass might support traditional, commercial, and habitat objectives. Although low-severity burns were historically used for beargrass habitat management, a century of fire suppression has contributed to site conditions where such burns are no longer feasible and high-severity fire is more likely to occur.

- Empirical information on the frequency, intensity, and severity of fire in beargrass ecosystems is modest, but increasing in parts of the range of the plant. Traditional ecological knowledge associated with fire and fire effects is an additional source of information for beargrass management, but as it is specific to a time and a place, may be irrelevant for beargrass management today, and should be evaluated before implemented.

- Current management practices treat beargrass as a product rather than as part of an ecosystem. Local management decisions will depend greatly on beargrass population characteristics, local resource needs, pollinator needs, and site-specific factors such as topography, fuel build-up, fuel types and diversity, and fire history of both burn sites and adjacent areas.

Research Needs and Opportunities

Effects of human disturbances in beargrass habitat—
Harvesting overstory trees—Relationships among different harvest and silvicultural systems and beargrass survival, growth, and reproduction are understudied. The harvest of overstory trees would create canopy openings to increase light levels and soil temperatures, which could stimulate beargrass growth and sexual reproduction.

Harvesting beargrass leaves—Few studies have been conducted on the ecological effects of harvesting nontimber forest products such as beargrass. Empirical evidence is lacking, for example, on whether leaving tillers during leaf harvest prevents subsequent flowering of the plant. In general, loss of leaves directly decreases the amount of photosynthetic tissue in a plant and thereby reduces its resources available for growth, reproduction, and survival (Cardel and Koptur 2010). Potential responses of leaf loss could include changes in resource allocation (affecting flowering) and changes in the quality and number of pollen grains produced (Cardel and Koptur 2010). Heavy leaf harvest might also result in higher rates of plant mortality, which (combined with reduced flowering) could affect pollinators. The effect of beargrass harvest on its main pollinators is unknown.

Effects of natural disturbances in beargrass habitat—
Fire effects—The structural leaf differences between previously burned vs. unburned plants have not been investigated. The direct and indirect effects of fire on the pollinators of beargrass is not well understood.

Effects of landslides—The effect of landslides on the reproductive strategy and persistence of beargrass is not understood. The relative importance of vegetative verses sexual reproduction in beargrass varies with habitat characteristics, and flowering potential appears to be related to increased light levels and soil temperatures (Maule 1959).

Effects on plant reproduction—The persistence and viability of beargrass seed is unknown. Information is lacking on the relative effects of light conditions, underground competition, and changes in them on the reproductive strategy and fitness of beargrass. Furthermore, the nutritional value of beargrass pollen is poorly understood. As a rule, pollen resources high in protein are more valuable to pollinators by providing an essential nutrient in concentrated form, and by reducing the foraging strain on these insects. Pollen energy calculations at the habitat level could illuminate the role of beargrass in a plant community. Because pollen consumers occupy a low position in the food chain, and beargrass is often a dominant plant where it occurs, changes in the availability of beargrass pollen energy are not only important to pollinators, but may have cascading ecosystem effects.

Volume and value of beargrass leaves harvested—
No coordinated effort currently exists among landowners to monitor the volume of harvested material being removed from specific locations, or from larger regions. Instead, most monitoring efforts simply track the number of permits issued in a given year and enforcement of harvest limits is difficult. There is a lack of long-term price data within the floral greens industry as a whole and for beargrass specifically. Information on harvest levels and prices would improve the ability of landowners to set permit prices.

Potential Management Activities

The potential activities to manage beargrass for which peer-reviewed or other published material can inform their design and implementation fall into the categories of prescribed fire, manual clearing, reestablishment, and silviculture. Better monitoring of leaf harvests and markets could provide useful information about plant populations associated with management activities.

Prescribed fire—

The severity, frequency, and timing of wildfire differ across the range of beargrass (table 9), and all need to be considered in designing and conducting prescribed burns. On the Six Rivers National Forest in California, for example, a prescribed-burn target of .8094 ha (2 ac) per year was used to promote plants for traditional harvest, and the burns were conducted during the regular fire season on one-tenth to one-fourth-acre plots (Hunter 1988). According to Peter and Shebitz (2006), a fire-return interval of less than 20 years may be necessary to have long-lasting effects on beargrass reproduction and growth. This frequency would likely limit shrub and tree encroachment and ensure enough time for long leaves of basketmaking and commercial quality to develop (Shebitz et al. 2009a). Rentz (2003) documented increased pliability in beargrass leaves 2 years postfire. For prescribed fire related to basketry, Hunter (1998) recommended a fire that burns 75 to 95 percent of living beargrass foliage in addition to 90 to 100 percent of old, dry growth. According to Hunter (1988), a highly specific fire behavior is not essential to produce good results in beargrass, as long as the desired consumption is obtained and the fire is held within control lines. Flame lengths of .23 m to .91m (.75 to 3 ft) and a rate of spread between .30 m and 1.21 m (1 to 4 ft) per minute have produced acceptable results (Hunter 1988). In general, very high temperatures and long residence times associated with heavy fuel concentrations are most likely to cause beargrass mortality, and low-severity fires have been historically used for beargrass habitat management (Hunter 1988, Peter and Shebitz 2006). Damp weather conditions may also help limit fire severity. Under wet or moist conditions, the moisture held in the basal leaves will limit the transfer of heat to the meristem, but under dry conditions, leaves may increase the heat delivered to the base of the rosette. If beargrass tussocks have accumulated leaf litter, they may continue to burn after a fire passes, further increasing the likelihood of meristematic damage and plant mortality (Shebitz et al. 2009a).

Manual clearing—

The cutting of shrubs and trees may be a useful management approach for restoring and maintaining pollinator habitat, either alone or in combination with fire. Relative to burning, the mechanical removal of vegetation may be less risky for pollinators, in that pollinator habitat is promoted without the temporary destruction of herbaceous food and habitat resources (Mader et al. 2011). However, this management type has been rarely studied, and, according to a review by Swengel (2001), little research is available for comparing tree cutting and other management in a pollinator conservation context.

Reestablishment—

The three most promising techniques for reestablishing beargrass are direct seeding, transplanting greenhouse-grown seedlings, and transplanting wild-harvested seedlings. Both wild-collected seeds and greenhouse grown plants are commercially available. Shebitz et al. (2009a) had the greatest success direct seeding into severely burned habitat with mineral soil exposed (relative to unburned and lightly burned conditions).

Silviculture—

A silvicultural system is a planned series of treatments for a forest stand that implies a process for creating target conditions over time. The timing and intensity of treatments in any system that are designed to manage forest ecosystem diversity in the range of beargrass will depend on site-specific conditions as well as on the key management objectives. Clearcutting is an even-age system that removes almost all trees, creating a fully exposed microclimate for a new age class of trees to develop. In the Pacific Northwest, clearcutting predominated for a century (Curtis et al. 1998, Tesch 1994). The system might provide sufficient light to stimulate flowering in beargrass, but could adversely affect the structural properties of soil and the quantities of dead wood associated with adequate drainage and with pollinator habitat. As an alternative, a two-age, shelterwood system could create the dappled light environment that promotes flowering in beargrass, leaf properties suitable for traditional harvesters, and standing dead and down wood for decomposers. A shelterwood is one in which most trees are harvested, but some are left to shade the new trees establishing underneath. It involves the intentional use of shade, which can give desired species a growth advantage over competing vegetation during the establishment phase of regeneration. Trees retained in a shelterwood system are generally harvested after a new age class is established. In contrast to even-age or two-age systems, an uneven-age system regenerates a forest stand with three or more age classes. This is typically accomplished with some form of selection system. In these systems, mature and immature trees are felled to create or maintain uneven-age stands. Single tree selection fells individual trees and generally tends to increase the proportion of shade-tolerant species in mixed-species stands. Group selection cuts trees in units and therefore maintains a higher proportion of shade-intolerant species in mixed-species stands than individual tree selection. Uneven-age systems would likely create a shadier environment that inhibited beargrass flowering but produced leaf properties desired by commercial harvesters. They would also tend to promote dead and down wood for decomposers. We did not find published studies on the effects of different silvicultural systems or intensities of harvest specifically on beargrass. Variable retention harvesting, which creates gaps and groups of multiaged forest, may favor beargrass populations by providing a gradient of light between tree and shrub seral stages. Such conditions could produce the "filtered" light that promotes leaf elongation suitable to tribal and commercially desired leaf morphology.

In addition to bare ground, dead wood is a critical resource for many pollinators. The larvae of most pollinating beetles (e.g., *Cosmosalia chrysocoma*) and some syrphid flies (e.g., *Cheilosia hoodiana*) require dead wood for food and habitat, and the abundance of these pollinators in a given habitat is known to increase with abundance of dead wood (e.g., Ferrenberg et al. 2006, Reemer 2005). Thus, managed beargrass sites should include an abundance and diversity of dead wood, including stumps, standing snags, and fallen logs, and piles of logs or brush, all of which are important pollinator resources (Mader et al. 2011). It should be noted that the larval food requirements of pollinators with predaceous larval stages (e.g., *Parasyrphus* syrphid flies and *Epicauta* blister beetles) will be best met by promoting a diversity of flowering plants, because prey species are often herbivorous (or predatory on herbivores) (Mader et al. 2011).

Restricting or monitoring beargrass harvests—
Plant death and damage can occur as a result of overharvest or careless harvest practices. Education of harvesters to encourage less-destructive gathering practices (particularly with regard to meristem damage) may help reduce damage to a beargrass population. Measures like restricting the number of leaves that can be harvested from an individual plant, or the frequency that a given population can be harvested, may be warranted in some locations. However, such restrictions are nearly impossible to enforce, and these goals might be best achieved through education or self-monitoring. According to Charnley et al. (2008), many experienced floral-greens harvesters in the Pacific Northwest already adhere to self-imposed harvest level restrictions, and practice resource rotation that allows areas to lie fallow and recover for future harvest. Harvesters may also be willing to participate in productivity experiments or techniques (such as monitoring flowering behavior or spreading beargrass seeds) particularly if these activities are aimed at sustaining the livelihoods of harvesters over the long term (Charnley et al. 2008). Any educational

materials (as well as any signage or regulatory information) should be published in languages other than English, in which not all harvesters are fluent.

Harvest might also be better managed by efforts to regulate and better meet consumer demand. Developing cold storage facilities or spreading out processing facilities would enable the floral greens industry to profitably sell purchased greens for longer periods of time, and presumably help regulate the prices paid to harvesters and distribute benefits across a wider range of communities. The creation of cooperatives might enable harvesters to develop relationships with individual buying sheds with better benefit sharing; better benefits might lessen the harvest pressure. The use of stewardship contracts over permits might also enable landowners to share the burden of habitat maintenance with harvesters.

Conserving Beargrass Ecosystem Diversity

Best management practices to conserve ecosystem diversity will differ according to local disturbance regimes within a regional context. What does this mean for ecosystem management to achieve conservation? One implication is that management needs and approaches will differ throughout the range of beargrass because ecosystem values at risk in one location may be less of a concern elsewhere. For example, concerns about insufficient beargrass leaves for Indian basketry are documented in the Pacific Northwest, but not in the Rocky Mountains. This same principle likely applies to a number of other species as well.

Because management needs and approaches are likely to differ locally within the range of beargrass there is a role for traditional and local ecological knowledge, in addition to western scientific knowledge, in contributing to ecosystem conservation, especially when a threatened value is sociocultural in nature. We define traditional ecological knowledge as a cumulative body of knowledge about the relationships between people, other living things, and the environment that is handed down across generations through cultural transmission (Berkes 2000). In includes knowledge, practices, beliefs, and the range of skills and strategies that people use to respond to the environmental circumstances in which they find themselves (Berkes 1999). It is dynamic and changes over time as people adapt to changing environmental conditions, experiment, build on their experiences and observations, and interact with other knowledge systems. It is also place-based. Similarly, local ecological knowledge includes knowledge, practices, beliefs, skills, and strategies that people develop as a result of extensive interactions with, and personal observation of, local ecosystems (Charnley et al. 2007). This knowledge is more recent, and may eventually become traditional ecological knowledge. There are several examples of how traditional and local ecological knowledge can be integrated into biodiversity conservation efforts (see Charnley et al. 2007, 2008). A desirable way is to engage the knowledge holders directly, as active participants in conservation efforts, using participatory approaches. One important implication regarding the use of local ecological knowledge within conservation planning is the fact that local ecological knowledge is specific to a time and place (Gadgil et al. 1993, Gilchrist and Mallory 2007, Vance et al. 2001). It is, therefore, important to evaluate and supplement this knowledge with scientific experimentation.

References

Adams, A.B.; Dale, V.H.; Smith, E.P.; Kruckeberg, A.R. 1987. Plant survival, growth form and regeneration following the 18 May 1980 eruption of Mount St. Helens, Washington. Northwest Science. 61(3): 160–170.

Agee, J.K. 1993. Fire ecology of the Pacific Northwest. Washington, DC: Island Press. 493 p.

University of Michigan-Dearborn. 2003. Native American Ethnobotany: A database of food, drugs, dyes and fibers of Native American peoples, derived from plants. (17 January 2011).

Anderson, M.K. 2005. Tending the wild: Native American knowledge and the management of California's natural resources. Berkeley, CA: University of California Press. 555 p.

Anzinger, D.; Radosevich, S.R. 2008. Fire and nonnative invasive plants in the Northwest coastal bioregion. In: Zouhar, K.; Smith, J.K.; Sutherland, S.; Brooks, M.L., eds. Wildland fire in ecosystems: fire and nonnative invasive plants. Gen. Tech. Rep. RMRS-GTR-42-vol. 6. Ogden, UT: U.S. Department of Agriculture, Forest Service, Rocky Mountain Research Station. 354–355.

Arnett, R.H., Jr.; Thomas, M.C.; Skelley, P.E.; Frank, J.H., eds. 2002. American Beetles, Volume II: Polyphaga: Scarabaeoidea through Curculionoidea. Boca Raton, FL: CRC Press. 881 p.

Arno, S.F.; Simmerman, D.G.; Keane, R.E. 1985. Forest succession on four habitat types in western Montana. Gen. Tech. Rep. INT-177. Ogden, UT: U.S. Department of Agriculture, Forest Service, Intermountain Forest and Range Experiment Station. 74 p.

ATADA. 2004. The Antique Tribal Art Dealers Association, Inc. Media files: Some twists in the old-new basketmaker's art. http://www.atada.org/2004_Media_Files.html. (17 January 2011).

Bakhle, A. 2009. The art of Native American basketry: A living tradition. Fabrik Magazine. http://www.fabrikmagazine.com/content/the-art-of-native-american-basketry-a-living-tradition/. (1 December 2010).

Barbour, M.G.; Minnich. R.A. 2000. California upland forests and woodlands. In: Barbour, M.G.; Billings, W.D., eds., North American terrestrial vegetation, 2nd ed. Cambridge, United Kingdom: Cambridge University Press: 161–202.

Barrett, S.W.; Arno, S.F. 1999. Indian fires in the Northern Rockies; ethnohistory and ecology. In: Boyd, R., ed., Indians, fire, and the land in the Pacific Northwest. Corvallis, OR: Oregon State University Press: 50–64.

Barrett, S.; Helenurm, K. 1987. The reproductive biology of forest herbs: 1. Breeding systems and pollination. Canadian Journal of Botany. 65(10): 2036–2046.

Bartuszvige, A.M.; Kennedy, P.L. 2009. Synthesis of knowledge on the effects of fire and thinning treatments on understory vegetation in U.S. dry forests. Special Report 1095. Extension and Experiment Station Communications. Corvallis, OR: Oregon State University. http://www.firescience.gov/projects/07-S-11/project/07-S-11_07_s_11_fire_thinning_effects_understory_vegetation.pdf. (22 Febuary 2011).

Battles, J.J.; Shlisky, A.J.; Barrett, R.H.; Heald, R.C.; Allen-Diaz, B.H. 2001. The effects of forest management on plant species diversity in a Sierran conifer forest. Forest Ecology and Management. 146(1–3): 211–222.

Bennett, R.S.; Shaw, C.R. 1987. Basketmaking among the Karuk. Arcata, CA: Humboldt State University Center for Community Development. 45 p.

Berkes, F., 1999. Sacred ecology: traditional ecological knowledge and resource management. Philadelphia, PA: Taylor and Francis. 209 p.

Berkes, F.; Colding, J.; Folke, C. 2000. Rediscovery of traditional ecological knowledge as adaptive management. Ecological Applications. 10(5): 1251–1262.

Bernhardt, P. 2000. Convergent evolution and adaptive radiation of beetle-pollinated angiosperms. Plant Systematics and Evolution. 222: 293–320.

Bernhardt, P. 2011. Personal communication. Pollinator biologist, Department of Biology, St. Louis University, 221 N. Grand Ave., St. Louis, MO 63103.

Bernhardt, P.; Thien, L.B. 1987. Self-isolation and insect pollination in the primitive angiosperms: new evaluations of older hypotheses. Plant Systematics and Evolution. 156: 159–176.

Black, S.A.; Hodges, N.; Vaughan, M.; Shepherd, M. 2007. Pollinators in natural areas: a primer on habitat management. Portland, OR: Xerces Society for Invertebrate Conservation. 8 p.

Black, S.A.; Vaughan, M.; Shepherd, M. 2011. Rangeland management for pollinators. Rangelands. 33(3): 9–13. http://www.bione.org/doi/full/10.2111/155-501x-33.3.9. (11 January 2012).

Blatner, A.K.; Alexander, S. 1998. Recent price trends for non-timber forest products in the Pacific Northwest. Forest Products Journal. 48(10): 28–34.

Boyd, R. 1999. Indians, fire, and the land in the Pacific Northwest. Corvallis, OR: Oregon State University Press. 313 p.

Brockway, D.G.; Topik, C.; Hemstrom, M.A.; Emmingham, W.H. 1983. Plant association and management guide for the Pacific silver fir zone—Gifford Pinchot National Forest. R6-Ecol-130a-1983. Portland, OR: U.S. Department of Agriculture, Forest Service, Pacific Northwest Region. 122 p.

Brooks, M.L. 2008. Plant invasions and fire regimes. In: Zouhar, K.; Smith, J.K.; Sutherland, S.; Brooks M.L. eds., Wildland fire in ecosystems: fire and nonnative invasive plants. Gen. Tech. Rep. RMRS-GTR-42-vol. 6. Ogden, UT: U.S. Department of Agriculture, Forest Service, Rocky Mountain Research Station. 355 p.

Brotherton, B., ed. 2008. S'abadeb, the gifts: Pacific Coast Salish art and artists. Seattle, WA: University of Washington Press. 240 p.

Brown, B.A. 2001. Challenges facing community forestry: the role of low income forest workers. Research Bulletin 2. Wolf Creek, OR: Jefferson Center for Education and Research. 7 p.

Brown, B.A.; Marin-Hernandez, A. eds. 2000. Voices from the woods: lives and experiences of non-timber forest workers. Wolf Creek, OR: Jefferson Center for Education and Research. 52 p.

Burke, H.E. 1905. Black check in western hemlock. Bureau of Entomology Circular No. 61. Washington, DC: U.S. Department of Agriculture. 10 p.

Calflora, 2011. Information on California plants for education, research and conservation, based on data contributed by dozens of public and private institutions and individuals, including the Consortium of Calif. Herbaria. [web application]. Berkeley, CA: The Calflora Database. http://www.calflora.org/. (4 February 2011).

California Baskets. 2011. CaliforniaBaskets.com: specializing in Northern California Indian baskets. http://www.californiabaskets.com/consignmentbaskets. htm. (20 January 2011).

Campbell, J.W.; Hanula, J.L.; Waldrop, T.A. 2007. Effects of prescribed fire and fire surrogates on floral visiting insects of the blue ridge province in North Carolina. Biological Conservation. 134: 393–404.

Capinera, J.L., ed. 2008. Encyclopedia of entomology, 2nd ed. Vols. 1–4. The Netherlands: Springer, Dordrecht. 4346 p. http://books.google.com/ books?id=i9ITMiiohVQC. (16 February 2011).

Cardel, Y.; Koptur, S. 2010. Effects of florivory on the pollination of flowers: an experimental field study with a perennial plant. International Journal of Plant Science. 171(3): 283–292.

Charnley, S.; Fischer, A.P.; Jones, E.T. 2007. Integrating traditional and local ecological knowledge into forest biodiversity conservation in the Pacific Northwest. Forest Ecology and Management. 246(1): 14–28.

Charnley, S.; Fischer, A.P.; Jones, E.T. 2008. Traditional and local ecological knowledge about forest biodiversity in the Pacific Northwest Gen. Tech. Rep. PNW-GTR-751. U.S. Department of Agriculture, Forest Service, Pacific Northwest Research Station. 52 p.

Coe, R.T. 1986. Lost and found traditions: Native American art, 1965–1985. Seattle, WA: University of Washington Press. 288 p.

Cole, F.R. 1969. The flies of western North America. Berkeley, CA: University of California Press. 693 p. http://www.phorid.net/flower_fly/hover_species_pages/ cheilosia_hoodiana.htm. (2 January 2011).

Collins, B.; Foré, S. 2009. Potential role of pollinators in microhabitat structure within a large population of *Echinacea laevigata* (Asteraceae). The Journal of the Torrey Botanical Society. 136(4): 445–456.

Craighead, F.C. 1923. North American cerambycid larvae: a classification and the biology of North American cerambycid larvae. Canada Department of Agriculture Entomological Bulletin. 23: 1–239. http://www.archive.org/stream/no rthamericancer00craiuoft#page/94/mode/2up. (17 February 2011).

Crane, M.F. 1990. *Xerophyllum tenax*. Fire Effects Information System. U.S Department of Agriculture, Forest Service, Rocky Mountain Research Station. http://www.fs.fed.us/database/feis/plants/forbs/xerten/all.html. (10 December 2010).

Curtis, R.O.; DeBell, D.S.; Harrington, C.A.; Lavender, D.P.; St. Clair, J.B.; Tappeiner, J.C.; Walstad, J.D. 1998. Silviculture for multiple objectives in the Douglas-fir region. Gen. Tech. Rep. PNW-GTR-435. Portland, OR: U.S. Department of Agriculture, Forest Service, Pacific Northwest Research Station. 123 p.

Dekker-Robertson, D.; Griessmann, P.; Baumgartner, D.; Hanley, D. [N.d.]. Forest Health Notes: Annosus root disease. Pullman, WA: Washington State University Cooperative Extension. http://ext.nrs.wsu.edu/forestryext/foresthealth/notes/annosusrootdisease.htm. (14 February 2011).

Dobson, H.E.M. 2006. Relationship between floral fragrance composition and type of pollinator. In: Dudareva, N.; Pichersky, E., eds. Biology of floral scent. Boca Raton, FL: CRC Press: 147–198.

Drabble, E.; Drabble, H. 1917. The Syrphid visitors to certain flowers. New Phytologist. 16(5/6): 105–109.

Draffan G. 2006. Endgame research. http://www.endgame.org/index.html. (13 February 2012).

Drees, B.M.; Jackman, J. 1999. Field guide to Texas insects. Houston, TX: Gulf Publishing Company. http://insects.tamu.edu/fieldguide/bimg167.html. (1 March 2011).

Dyrness, C.T. 1965. The effect of logging and slash burning on understory vegetation in the H.J. Andrews Experimental Forest. Res. Note PNW-31. Portland, OR: U.S. Department of Agriculture, Forest Service, Pacific Northwest Forest and Range Experiment Station. 13 p.

Eberling, H.; Olesen, J.M. 1999. The structure of a high latitude plant-flower visitor system: the dominance of flies. Ecography. 22: 314–323.

Fall, H.C.; Cockerell, T.D.A. 1907. The Coleoptera of New Mexico. Transactions of the American Entomological Society. (1890-) 33(2/3): 145–272.

Faegri, K.; van der Pijl, L. 1979. The principles of pollination ecology. 3rd ed. Oxford, United Kingdom: Pergamon Press. 244 p.

Fenster, C.B.; Armbruster, W.S.; Wilson, P.; Dudash, M.R.; Thomson, J.D. 2004. Pollination syndromes and floral specialization. Annual Review of Ecology and Systematics. 35: 375–403.

Ferrenberg, S.M.; Schwilk, D.W.; Knapp, E.E.; Groth, E.; Keeley, J.E. 2006. Fire decreases arthropod abundance but increases diversity: early and late season prescribed fire effects in a Sierra Nevada mixed-conifer forest. Fire Ecology. 2: 79–102.

Gadgil, M.; Berkes, F.; Folke, C. 1993. Indigenous knowledge for biodiversity conservation. Ambio. 22(2/3): 151–156.

Gao, J.K.; Butler, D.R. 1992. Terrain influences on total length of snow avalanche paths in southern Glacier National Park, Montana. The Geographical Bulletin. 34(2): 91–101.

Gilchrist, G.; Mallory, M.L. 2007. Comparing expert-based science with local ecological knowledge: what are we afraid of? Ecology and Society. 12(1): r1. [online]. http://www.ecologyandsociety.org/vol12/iss1/resp1/. (23 April 2012).

Goldsmith, S.K. 1987. Resource distribution and its effect on the mating system of a longhorned beetle, *Perarthrus linsleyi* (Coleoptera: Cerambycidae). Oecologia. 73(2): 317–320.

Gullan, P.J.; Cranston, P. 2010. The insects: an outline of entomology. London: John Wiley and Sons. 565 p.

Gunther, E. 1927. Klallam Ethnography. Seattle, WA: University of Washington Publications in Anthropology. 1(5).

Gunther, E. 1973. Ethnobotany of western Washington: the knowledge and use of indigenous plants by Native Americans. Seattle, WA: University of Washington Press. 74 p.

Haddock, R.C.; Chaplin, S.D. 1982. Pollination and seed production in two phenologically divergent prairie legumes (*Baptisia leucophaea* and *B. leucantha*). American Midland Naturalist. 108(1): 175–186.

Hagle, S.K.; Gibson, K.E.; Tunnock, S. 2003. A field guide to diseases, insect pests of northern central Rocky Mountain conifers. U.S. Department of Agriculture, Forest Service, Northern and Intermountain Regions. http://www.fs.fed.us/r1-r4/spf/fhp/field_guide/index.htm. (14 Febuary 2010).

Halpern, C.B.; Spies, T.A. 1995. Plant species diversity in natural and managed forests of the Pacific Northwest. Ecological Applications. 5(4): 913–934.

Hansis, R. 1996. The harvesting of special forest products by Latinos and southeast Asians in the Pacific Northwest: preliminary observations. Society and Natural Resources. 9: 611–615.

Hansis, R. 1998. A political ecology of picking: non-timber forest products in the Pacific Northwest. Human Ecology. 26(1): 67–86.

Harper, M.G.; Dietrich, C.H.; Larimore, R.L.; Tessene, P.E. 2000. Effects of prescribed fire on prairie arthropods: an enclosure study. Natural Areas Journal. 20: 325–335.

Hartley, M.K.; Rogers, W.E.; Siemann, E.; Grace, J. 2007. Responses of prairie arthropod communities to fire and fertilizer: balancing plant and arthropod conservation. American Midland Naturalist. 157: 92–105.

Hawkeswood, T.J.; Turner, J.R. 2007. Record of pollination of *Lomatia silaifolia* (Sm.) R.Br. (Proteaceae) by the longicorn beetle *Uracanthus triangularis* (Hope, 1833) (Coleoptera: Cerambycidae). Calodema Supplementary Paper. 53: 1–3.

Heffner, K. 1984. Following the smoke: contemporary plant procurement by the Indians of Northern California. Unpublished report. On file with : U.S. Department of Agriculture, Forest Service, Six Rivers National Forest, 1330 Bayshore Way, Eureka, CA 95501.

Higgins, S.; Blatner, K.; Kerns, B.K.; Worthington, A. 2004. Relationship between *Xerophyllum tenax* and canopy density in the southern Cascades of Washington. Western Journal of Applied Forestry. 19: 82–87.

Hitchcock, G.L.; Cronquist, A. 1973. Flora of the Pacific Northwest: an illustrated manual. Seattle, WA: University of Washington Press. 730 p.

Henderson, J.A.; Peter, D.H.; Lesher, R.D.; Shaw, D.C. 1989. Forested plant associations of the Olympic National Forest. R6-ECOL-TP-001-88. Portland, OR: U.S. Department of Agriculture, Forest Service, Pacific Northwest Region. 502 p.

Hunn, E.S. 1990. Nchi'i-Wana, the big river: Mid-Columbia Indians and their land. Seattle, WA: University of Washington Press: 378 p.

Hunter, J.E. 1988. Prescribed burning for cultural resources. Fire Management Notes. 49(2): 8–9.

Huntzinger, M. 2003. Effects of fire management practices on butterfly diversity in the forested western United States. Biological Conservation. 113: 1–12.

Hutchinson, G.E. 1953. The concept of pattern in ecology. Proceedings of the Academy of Natural Sciences of Philadelphia. 105: 1–12.

Johnson, S.D.; Horn, K.C.; Savage, A.M.; Windhager, S.; Simmons, M.T.; Rudgers, J.A. 2008. Timing of prescribed burns affects abundance and composition of arthropods in the Texas Hill Country. The Southwestern Naturalist. 53(2): 137–145.

Jones, S., ed. 1983. Pacific basket makers: a living tradition. Honolulu, HI: Consortium for Pacific Arts and Cultures. 80 p.

Kearns, C.A.; Inouye, D.W. 1997. Pollinators, flowering plants, and conservation biology. BioScience. 47: 297–307.

Kearns, C.A.; Inouye, D.W.; Waser, N. 1998. Endangered mutualisms: the conservation of plant-pollinator interactions. Annual Review of Ecology and Systematics. 29: 83–112.

Kearns, C.A. 1992. Anthophilous fly distribution across an elevation gradient. American Midland Naturalist. 127: 172–182.

Keeley, J.E.; Stephenson, H.L. 2000. Restoring natural fire regimes to the Sierra Nevada in an era of global climate change. In: Cole, D.N.; McCool, S.F.; Borrie, W.T.; McLoughlin, J., eds. Proceedings of the wilderness science in a time of change conference. RMRS-P-15. U.S. Department of Agriculture, Forest Service, Rocky Mountain Research Station: 255–265.

Kerr, J.T.; Packer, L. 1999. The environmental basis of North American species richness patterns among *Epicauta* (Coleoptera: Meloidae). Biodiversity and Conservation. 8: 617–628.

Kerstyn, A.; Stiling, P. 1999. The effects of burn frequency on the density of some grasshoppers and leaf miners in a Florida sandhill community. Florida Entomologist. 82: 499–505.

Kinney, K.; Peairs, F.B.; Swinker, A.M. 2010. Blister beetles in forage crops. Number 5.524. Colorado State University Extension. U.S. Department of Agriculture and Colorado Counties: http://www.ext.colostate.edu/pubs/insect/05524.html. (16 February 2011).

Klinger, R.C.; Underwood, E.C.; Moore, P.E. 2006. The role of environmental gradients in non-native plant invasions into burnt areas of Yosemite National Park, California. Diversity and Distributions. 12: 139–156.

Klinger, R.; Wills, R.; Brooks, M.L. 2008. Fire and nonnative invasive plants in the southwest coastal bioregion. In: Zouhar, K.; Smith, J.K.; Sutherland, S.; Brooks, M.L., eds. Wildland fire in ecosystems: fire and nonnative invasive plants. Gen. Tech. Rep. RMRS-GTR-42-vol. 6. Ogden, UT: U.S. Department of Agriculture, Forest Service, Rocky Mountain Research Station. 355 p.

Kremen, C.; Williams, N.M.; Aizen, M.A.; Gemmill-Herren, B.; LeBuhn, G.; Minckley, R.; Packer, L.; Potts, S.G.; Roulston, T.; Steffan-Dewenter, I.; Vázquez, D.P.; Winfree, R.; Adams, L.; Crone, E.E.; Greenleaf, S.S.; Keitt, T.H.; Klein, A.-M.; Regetz, J.; Ricketts, T.H. 2007. Pollination and other ecosystem services produced by mobile organisms: a conceptual framework for the effects of land-use change. Ecology Letters. 10: 299–314.

Kramer, B. 2001. Dangerous harvests? Natural resources: Forest Service studying whether popularity of beargrass is harming ecosystem. The Spokesman-Review. June 5. http://www.spokesmanreview.com/newsstory. asp?date=060501&ID=s973531. (3 December 2010).

Kruckeberg, A. 2003. Gardening with native plants of the Pacific Northwest. Seattle, WA: University of Washington Press. 288 p.

Lake, F. 2011. Karuk story: Frog woman and beargrass, an adaptation. Personal communication. Research ecologist, U.S. Department of Agriculture, Forest Service, Pacific Southwest Research Station, 1700 Bayview Dr., Arcata, CA 95521.

LaLande, J.; Pullen, R. 1999. Burning for a "fine and beautiful open country;" native uses of fire in southwestern Oregon. In: Boyd, R., ed. Indians, fire, and the land in the Pacific Northwest. Corvallis, OR: Oregon State University Press: 185–218.

Larson, B.M.H.; Kevan, P.G.; Inouye, D.W. 2001. Flies and flowers: taxonomic diversity of anthophiles and pollinators. Canadian Entomologist. 133: 439–465.

Lau, T.C.; Stephenson, A.G. 1993. Effects of soil nitrogen on pollen production, pollen grain size, and pollen performance in *Cucurbita pepo* (Cucurbitaceae). American Journal of Botany. 80: 763–780.

Lau, T.C.; Stephenson, A.G. 1994. Effects of soil phosphorus on pollen production, pollen size, pollen phosphorus content, and the ability to sire seeds in *Cucurbita pepo* (Cucurbitaceae). Sexual Plant Reproduction. 7: 215–220.

Laursen, S.B. 1984. Predicting shrub community composition and structure following management disturbance in forest ecosystems of the Intermountain West. Moscow, ID: University of Idaho. 261 p. Ph.D. dissertation.

Lobb, A. 1990. Indian baskets of the Pacific Northwest and Alaska. Portland, OR: Graphic Arts Center Publishing Co. 128 p.

Lynch, K.A.; McLain, R.J. 2003. Access, labor, and wild floral greens management in western Washington's forests. Gen. Tech. Rep. PNW-GTR-585. U.S Department of Agriculture, Forest Service. Portland, OR: Pacific Northwest Research Station. 61 p.

MacRae, T.C.; Rice, M.E. 2007. Biological and distributional observations on North American Cerambycidae (Coleoptera). The Coleopterists Bulletin. 61(2): 227–263.

Mader, E.; Shepherd, M.; Vaughan, M.; Black, S.; LeBuhn, G. 2011. Attracting native pollinators: protecting North America's bees and butterflies. North Adams, MA: Storey Publishing. 380 p.

Marr, J. 2008. Assimilation through education: Indian boarding schools of the Pacific Northwest. University of Washington Libraries. http://content.lib. washington.edu/aipnw/marr.html#boarding. (13 February 2012).

Matheson, A.; Buchmann, S.L.; O'Toole, C.; Westrich, P.; Williams, I.H. eds. 1996. The conservation of bees. Linnean Society Symposium Series No. 18. New York: Academic Press. 254 p.

Maule, S.M. 1959. *Xerophyllum tenax*, squawgrass, its geographic distribution and its behaviour on Mount Rainier, Washington. Madrono. 15: 39–48.

McGehey J.H. 1967. The biologies of two hemlock bark beetles in western Oregon. Corvallis, OR: Oregon State University. 101 p.

McLain, D.K. 1982. Behavioral and morphological correlates of male dominance and courtship persistence in the blister beetle *Epicauta pennsylvanica* (Coleoptera: Meloidae). American Midland Naturalist. 107(2): 396–403.

McLain, R.J.; Lynch, K.A. 2010. Managing floral greens in a globalized economy; resource tenure, labour relations and immigration policy in the Pacific Northwest, USA. In: Wild: product governance: finding policies that work for non-timber forest products. London: Earthscan. 265 p.

Monné, M.A.; Bezark, L.G., Comps. 2010. Checklist of the Cerambycidae, or longhorned beetles (Coleoptera) of the Western Hemisphere, 2010 Version. http:// plant.cdfa.ca.gov/byciddb/checklists/WestHemiCerambycidae2010.pdf. (16 February 2011).

Montana Outdoors 2010. Photograph of crab spider (Thomsidae) on beargrass inflorescence in Montana. http://montucky.wordpress.com/2008/06/29/tiny-neighbors/#comments. (12 March 2011).

Morrison, P.H.; Swanson, F.J. 1990. Fire history and pattern in a Cascade Range landscape. Gen. Tech. Rep. PNW-GTR-254. Portland, OR: U.S. Department of Agriculture, Forest Service, Pacific Northwest Research Station. 77 p.

Moretti, M.; De Bello, F.; Roberts, S.P.M.; Potts, S.G. 2009. Taxonomical vs. functional responses of bee communities to fire in two contrasting climatic regions. Journal of Animal Ecology. 78(1): 98–108.

Morse, L.E.; Kartesz, J.T.; Kutner, L.S. 1995. Native vascular plants. In: LaRoe, E.T.; Farris, G.S.; Puckett, C.E.; Doran, P.D.; Mac, M.J; eds. Our living resources: a report to the Nation on the distribution, abundance, and health of U.S. plants, animals and ecosystems. Washington, DC: U.S. Department of the Interior, National Biological Service: 205–209.

Munger, S.H. 2003. Common to this country: botanical discoveries of Lewis and Clark. New York: Artisan Publishers. 128 p.

Museum Informatics Project. 2011. Shapes and uses of California Indian basketry. University of California, Berkeley. http://www.mip.berkeley.edu/cilc/basket.html. (17 January 2011).

Mussulman, J. 2004. Luxuriant beargrass. http://www.lewis-clark.org/content/content-article.asp?ArticleID=1318. (2 January 2011).

National Indian Forest Resources Management Act. 25 U.S.C. 31, Supplement 3, 2006 edition. Section 3101. http://www.gpo.gov/fdsys/pkg/USCODE-2010-title25/pdf/USCODE-2010-title25-chap33-sec3101.pdf. (28 September 2011).

National Research Council. 2006. Status of pollinators in North America. Washington, DC: The National Academies Press. 307 p.

O'Neale, L.M. 1928 [reprinted 1995]. Yurok-Karok basket weavers. Berkeley, CA: Phoebe Hearst Museum of Anthropology. 184 p.

O'Neale, L.M. 1930. North America: coiled basketry in British Columbia and surrounding region. American Anthropologist. 32(2): 306–308.

O'Neale, L.M. **1932.** Yurok-Karok basket weavers, Berkeley, CA: University of California Press: University of California Publications in Archaeology and Ethnology.

O'Neill, K.M.; Fultz, J.E.; Ivie, M.A. **2008.** Distribution of adult Cerambycidae and Buprestidae (Coleoptera) in a subalpine forest under shelterwood management. The Coleopterists Bulletin. 62(1): 27–36.

O'Toole, C.; Raw, A. **1991.** Bees of the world. London: Blandford Publishing. 192 p.

Owen, J.; Gilbert, F.S. **1989.** On the abundance of hoverflies (Syrphidae). Oikos. 55(2): 183–193.

Peet, R.K. **2000.** Forests and meadows of the Rocky Mountains. In: Barbour, M.G.; Billings, W.D, eds. North American Special Report 1095 37. Terrestrial vegetation. 2nd ed. Cambridge, United Kingdom: Cambridge University Press: 75–122.

Pendleton, R.L.; Pendleton, B.K.; Wetherill, K.R.; Griswold, T. **2008.** Reproductive biology of *Larrea tridentata*: a preliminary comparison between core shrubland and isolated grassland plants at the Sevilleta National Wildlife Refuge, New Mexico. In: Kitchen, S.L.; Pendleton, R.L.; Monaco, T.A.; Vernon, J., comps. Shrublands under fire: disturbance and recovery in a changing world. 2006 Proceedings RMRS-P-52. Fort Collins, CO: U.S. Department of Agriculture, Forest Service, Rocky Mountain Research Station: 131–135.

Peter, D. **2011.** The Skokomish savanna and woodlands vegetation survey: historical perspective and current status of an Olympic National Forest restoration project. Olympia, WA: Resilience and Ecosystem Disturbance Team. U.S Department of Agriculture, Forest Service, Pacific Northwest Research Station: 44 p.

Peter, D.; Shebitz, D.J. **2006.** Historic anthropogenically maintained bear grass savannas of the southeastern Olympic Peninsula. Restoration Ecology. 14(4): 605–615.

Pimentel, D.; Zuniga, R.; Morrison, D. **2005.** Update on the environmental and economic cost associated with alien-invasive species in the United States. Ecological Economics. 52: 273–288.

Pojar, J.; MacKinnon, A. **1994.** Plants of the Pacific Northwest coast: Washington, Oregon, British Columbia, and Alaska. Vancouver, BC: Lone Pine Publishing. 528 p.

Potts, S.G.; Vulliamy, B.; Dafni, A.; Ne'eman, G.; O'Toole, C.; Roberts, S.; Willmer, P. 2003. Response of plant-pollinator communities to fire: changes in diversity, abundance and floral reward structure. Oikos. 101: 103–112.

Pullen. R.J. 1996. Overview of the environment of native inhabitants of southwestern Oregon, late prehistoric era. Medford, OR: U.S Department of the Interior, Bureau of Land Management, Medford District Office. http://soda.sou.edu/awdata/021204a1.pdf. (25 April 2012).

Ramel, G. 1995. The social bees: Apidae. The Earth Life Web.net: http://www.earthlife.net/insects/socbees.html. (12 February 2011).

Randall, J.M.; Rejmánek, M.; Hunter, J.C. 1998. Characteristics of the exotic flora of California. Fremontia. 26(4): 3–12.

Rank, N.E.; Smiley, J.T. 1994. Host-plant effects on *Parasyrphus melanderi* Curran (Diptera: Syrphidae) feeding on a willow leaf beetle *Chrysomela aeneicollis* Schaeffer (Coleoptera: Chrysomelidae). Ecological Entomology. 19: 31–38.

Reemer, M. 2005. Saproxylic hoverflies benefit by modern forest management (Diptera: Syrphidae). Journal of Insect Conservation. 9: 49–59.

Rejmánek, M. 1989. Invasibility of plant communities. In: Drake, J.A.; Mooney, H.A.; DiCastri, F.; Groves, R.H.; Kruger, F.J.; Rejmánek, M.; Williamson, M., eds. Biological invasions: a global perspective. New York: John Wiley and Sons: 369–388.

Rentz, E. 2003. Effects of fire on plant anatomical structure in native Californian basketry materials. San Francisco, CA: San Francisco State University. 99 p. M.S thesis.

Rixen, C.; Haag, S.; Kulakowski, D.; Bebi, P. 2007. Natural avalanche disturbance shapes plant diversity and species composition in subalpine forest belt. Journal of Vegetation Science. 18: 735–742.

Robertson, C. 1929. Flowers and insects. Lancaster, PA: Science Press Printing Company: 221 p.

Roulston, T.H.; Cane, J.H.; Buchmann, S.L. 2000. What governs protein content of pollen: pollinator preferences, pollen-pistil interactions, or phylogeny? Ecological Monographs. 70(4): 617–643.

Rudall, P.J.; Stobart, K.L.; Hong, W.P.; Conran, J.G.; Furness, C.A. 2000. Consider the lilies: Systematics of Liliales. In: Wilson, K.L; Morrison, D.A, eds. Monocots: systematics and evolution. Collingwood, Australia: Csiro Publishing: 347–357.

Saab, V.; Block, W.; Russell, R.; Lehmkuhl, J.; Bate, L.; White, R. 2007. Birds and burns of the interior West: descriptions, habitats, and management in western forests. Gen. Tech. Rep. PNW-GTR-712. Portland, OR: U.S. Department of Agriculture, Forest Service, Pacific Northwest Research Station. 23 p.

Sage, T.L.; Pontieri, V.; Christopher, R. 2000. Incompatibility and mate recognition in monocotyledons. In: Wilson, K.L; Morrison, D.A. eds. Monocots: systematics and evolution. Collingwood, Australia: Csiro Publishing: 270–276.

Sapir, E.; Spier, L. 1943. Notes on the Culture of the Yana. Anthropological Records. 3(3): 252–253.

Schlick, M.D. 1994. Columbia River basketry: gift of the ancestors, gift of the Earth. Seattle, WA: University of Washington Press. 232 p.

Schlosser, W.E.; Blatner, K.A. 1997. Special forest products: an eastside perspective. Gen. Tech. Rep. PNW-GTR-380. Portland, OR: U.S. Department of Agriculture, Forest Service, Pacific Northwest Research Station. 35 p.

Schlosser, W.E.; Blatner, K.A.; Chapman, R.C. 1991. Economic and marketing implications of special forest products harvest in the coastal Pacific Northwest. Western Journal of Applied Forestry. 6(3): 67–72.

Schlosser, W.E.; Blatner, K.A.; Zamora, B. 1992. Pacific Northwest forest lands potential for forest greenery production. Northwest Science. 66(1): 44–55.

Senos, R.; Lake, F.L.; Turner, N.; Martinez, D. 2006. Traditional ecological knowledge and restoration practice. In: Apostol, D.; Sinclair, M. eds. Restoring the Pacific Northwest: The art and science of ecological restoration in Cascadia. Washington, DC: Island Press: 393–426.

Shebitz, D.J. 2005. Weaving traditional ecological knowledge into the restoration of basketry plants. Journal of Ecological Anthropology. 9: 51–68.

Shebitz, D. 2010. Personal communication. Plant ecologist, Kean University, Department of Biological Sciences, 1000 Morris Avenue, Union, NJ 07083.

Shebitz, D.J.; Reichard, S.H.; Woubneh, K. 2008. Beargrass (*Xerophyllum tenax*) on the Olympic Peninsula, Washington: autecology and population status. Northwest Science. 82(2): 128–140.

Shebitz, D.J.; Reichard, S.H.; Dunwiddie, P.W. 2009a. Ecological and cultural significance of burning beargrass habitat on the Olympic Peninsula, Washington. Ecological Restoration. 27(3): 306–319.

Shebitz, D.J.; Ewing, K.; Gutierrez, J. 2009b. Preliminary observations of using smokewater to increase low-elevation beargrass (*Xerophyllum tenax*) germination. Native Plants 10(1): 13–19.

Shebitz, D. J.; Kimmerer, R.W. 2005. Re-establishing roots of a Mohawk community and a culturally significant plant: sweetgrass. Restoration Ecology. 13: 257–264.

Storm, J. 1985. Quinault culture: Charlotte Kalama, basketmaker. Tahola, WA: Quinault Natural Resources.

Sullivan, W. 2009. Eye of the storm: Canyon Creek is a green oasis in the midst of the B&B burn. Eugene, OR: The Register-Guard. August 4. http://special.registerguard.com/csp/cms/sites/web/sports/outdoors/18109967-41/story.csp. (25 April 2012).

Sutherland, C.A. 2006. Wood boring beetles. O&T Guide [O-#10]. New Mexico State University, Cooperative Extension Service. http://aces.nmsu.edu/ces/plantclinic/documents/o-10-woodborers.pdf. (1 March 2011).

Swanson, F.J.; Dyrness, C.T. 1975. Impact of clear-cutting and road construction on soil erosion by landslides in the western Cascade Range, Oregon. Geology. 3(7): 393–396.

Swengel, A.B. 2001. A literature review of insect responses to fire, compared to other conservation managements of open habitat. Biodiversity and Conservation. 10: 1141–1169.

Takahashi, M.; Kawano, S. 1989. Pollen morphology of the Melanthiaceae and its systematic implications. Annals of the Missouri Botanical Garden. 76(3): 863–876.

Tepedino, V.J. 1979. The importance of bees and other insect pollinators in maintaining floral species composition. Great Basin Naturalist Memoirs. 3: 139–150.

Tesch, S.D. 1994. The Pacific Northwest region. In: Barrett, J.W., ed. Regional Silviculture of the United States, 3rd ed. New York: John Wiley & Sons: 499–599.

Thrush, C. 2007. Native Seattle: Histories from the crossing-over place. Seattle, WA: University of Washington Press. 326 p.

Thomas, M.G.; Schumann, D.R. 1993. Income opportunities in special forest products: self-help suggestions for rural entrepreneurs. Agric. Info. Bull. AIB-666. U.S. Department of Agriculture, Forest Service, State and Private Forestry. http://www.fpl.fs.fed.us/documnts/usda/agib666/aib666.pdf. (3 December 2010).

Turner, N.J. 1998. Plant technology of first peoples in British Columbia. Vancouver, BC: University of British Columbia Press. 288 p.

Turner, N.J.; Efrat, B.S. 1982. Ethnobotany of the Hesquiat Indians of Vancouver Island. Victoria, BC: British Columbia Provincial Museum. 101 p.

Turner, N.J.; Thomas, J.; Carlson, B.F.; Ogilvie, R.T. 1983. Ethnobotany of the Nitinaht Indians of Vancouver Island. Victoria, BC: British Columbia Provincial Museum. 87 p.

Turner, N.J.; Peacock, S. 2005. Solving the perennial paradox: ethnobotanical evidence for plant resource management on the Northwest Coast: management of plant species and habitats on the Northwest Coast. In: Deur, D.; Turner, N.J., eds. Keeping it living: traditions of plant use cultivation on the Northwest Coast of North America. Seattle, WA: University of Washington Press: 101–141.

U.S. Department of Agriculture, Forest Service [USDA FS]. 2011. PLANTS profile. *Xerophyllum tenax* (Pursh) Nutt., common beargrass. http://plants.U.S Department of Agriculutre, .gov/java/profile?symbol=XETE. (12 January 2011).

Vance, N.; Bernhardt, P.; Edens, R.M. 2004. Pollination and seed production in *Xerophyllum tenax* (Melanthiaceae) in the Cascade Range of central Oregon. American Journal of Botany. 91: 2060–2068.

Vance, N.C.; Borsting, M.; Pilz, D.; Freed, J. 2001. Special forest products: Species information guide for the Pacific Northwest. Gen. Tech. Rep. PNW-GTR-513. Portland, OR: U.S. Department of Agriculture, Forest Service, Pacific Northwest Research Station. 169 p.

Weigand, J. 2002. Overview of cultural traditions, economic trends, and key species in nontimber forest products of the Pacific Northwest. In: Jones, E.T.; McLain, R.J.; Weigand, J., eds. Nontimber forest products in the United States. Lawrence, KS: University of Kansas Press: 57–64.

Weems, H.V., Jr. 1954. Natural enemies and insecticides that are detrimental to beneficial Syrphidae. The Ohio Journal of Science. 54: 45–54.

Wheeler, W.M. 1908. Studies on myrmecophiles. Proceedings of the New York Entomological Society. Journal of the New York Entomological Society. 16(2): 115–124.

Werner, R.A. 2002. Effect of ecosystem disturbance on diversity of bark and wood-boring beetles (Coleoptera; Scolytidae, Burprestidae, Cerambycidae) in white spruce (*Picea glauca* (Moench) Voss) ecosystems of Alaska. Res. Pap. PNW-RP-546. Portland, OR; U.S Department of Agriculture, Forest Service, Pacific Northwest Research Station. 15 p.

Wick, D.; Evans, J.; Luna, T. 2008. Propagation protocol for production of container *Xerophyllum tenax* (Pursh) Nutt. plants (160 ml containers); U.S. Department of the Interior, National Park Service, Glacier National Park. http://www.nativeplantnetwork.org/Network/View/Protocols.aspx?protocolID=125. (29 December 2010).

Wray, J.; Anderson, M.K. 2003. Restoring Indian-set fires to prairie ecosystems on the Olympic Peninsula. Ecological Restoration. 21(4): 296–301.

Wright, C.S.; Agee, J.K. 2004. Fire and vegetation history in the eastern Cascade Mountains, Washington. Ecological Applications. 14(2): 443–459.

Yanega, D. 1996. Field guide to northeastern longhorn beetles (Coleoptera: Cerambycidae). Champaign, IL: Natural History Survey. 6: x + 1–174.

Young, H.J. 1988. Differential importance of beetle species pollinating *Dieffenbachia longispatha* (Araceae). Ecology. 69: 832–844.